Series Titles

Prehistory **I**	**XIII** Settling the Americas
Mesopotamia and the Bible Lands **II**	**XIV** Asian and African Empires
Ancient Egypt and Greece **III**	**XV** The Industrial Revolution
The Roman World **IV**	**XVI** Enlightenment and Revolution
Asian Civilizations **V**	**XVII** Nationalism and the Romantic Movement
Americas and the Pacific **VI**	**XVIII** The Age of Empire
Early Medieval Times **VII**	**XIX** North America: Expansion, Civil War, and Emergence
Beyond Europe **VIII**	
Late Medieval Europe **IX**	**XX** Turn of the Century and the Great War
Renaissance Europe **X**	**XXI** Versailles to World War II
Voyages of Discovery **XI**	**XXII** 1945 to the Cold War
Birth of Modern Nations **XII**	**XXIII** 1991 to the 21st Century
	XXIV Issues Today

Copyright © 2009 by McRae Books Srl, Florence (Italy)
This Zak Books edition was published in 2009.
Zak Books is an imprint of McRae Books Srl.

All rights reserved. No part of this book may be reproduced in any form without the prior written permission of the publisher and copyright owner.
All efforts have been made to obtain and provide compensation for the copyright to the photos and illustrations in this book in accordance with legal provisions. Persons who may nevertheless still have claims are requested to contact the copyright owners.

NORTH AMERICA: Expansion, Civil War and Emergence
was created and produced by McRae Books Srl
Via del Salviatino, 1 – 50016 – Florence (Italy)
info@mcraebooks.com
www.mcraebooks.com

Publishers: Anne McRae, Marco Nardi
Series Editor: Anne McRae
Author: Lisa Isenman
Main Illustrations: Francesca D'Ottavi pp. 9, 11, 20-21; Michela Gaudenzi pp. 44-45; MM comunicazione (Manuela Cappon, Monica Favilli, Gianni Sbragi, Cecilia Scutti) pp. 14-15, 18-19, 22-23, 25; Antonella Pastorelli pp. 42-43; Andrea Ricciardi di Gaudesi pp. 36-37.

Other illustrations: Studio Stalio (Alessandro Cantucci, Fabiano Fabbrucci, Margherita Salvadori)
Maps: Julian Baker
Photos: Bridgeman Art Library, London pp. 6-7b, 14a, 17, 22al, 25ar, 27a, 28-29b, 29al, 30ar, 31b, 32cl, 33b, 34al, 34br, 34-35c, 36br 36cl, 37ar, 38-39b, 38cl, 39ac, 40al, 41al, 43ac, 44ad, 44c; Di Novi / Columbia / The Kobal Collection / Joseph Lederer p. 41b; DK Images p. 40b; Getty Images p. 26ac; The Art Archive p. 7a.
Art Director: Marco Nardi
Layouts: Nick Leggett, Starry Dog Books Ltd
Project Editor and Research: Vicky Egan, Starry Dog Books Ltd
Repro: Litocolor, Florence

Consultant: Dr Ellen L. Berg
Associate Fellow, Rothermere American Institute, University of Oxford

Library of Congress Cataloging-in-Publication Data

North America: Expansion, Civil War and Emergence
ISBN 9788860981813

2009923562

Printed and bound in Malaysia.

HISTORY

North America:
Expansion, Civil War, and Emergence

Lisa Isenman

Consultant: Dr Ellen L. Berg
Associate Fellow, Rothermere American Institute, University of Oxford

Zak BOOKS

Contents

- 5 Introduction
- 6 Growth of a Modern Nation
- 8 The French and Barbary Wars
- 10 Lewis and Clark
- 12 The War of 1812
- 14 The Five Tribes
- 16 Texas and Mexico
- 18 The Trail of Tears
- 20 Gold and the Oregon Trail
- 22 White Southerners
- 24 Slavery and the Underground Railroad
- 26 The North: Factories and Cities
- 28 Civil War Breaks Out
- 30 Civil War: the Conclusion
- 32 Reconstruction Era
- 34 Native Americans Forced Out
- 36 Immigration
- 38 End of the Century: Money and Ideas
- 40 Art, Music, and Literature
- 42 Canada: Peoples and Rebellions
- 44 Canada: Union and Constitution
- 46 Glossary
- 47 Index

A Singer sewing machine from the 1850s.

TIMELINE

	1795	1800	1815	1830
Early Wars	The XYZ Affair sparks the Quasi War between the United States and France.	The Convention of 1800 ends America's alliance with France, which has existed since 1778.	British troops invade Washington D.C. and burn the White House.	Texas gains independence from Mexico in 1836.
Westward Expansion		In May, 1804, Lewis and Clark set off on their expedition to find a route to the West Coast.	From 1816 to 1821, six states were created: Indiana, Illinois, Maine, Mississippi, Alabama, and Missouri.	
Native Americans		Sequoyah develops his system for writing the Cherokee language.		Native Americans are moved west and their lands in the East are taken by white settlers.
Slavery Issues		In 1808 the foreign slave trade is made illegal and prices for slaves soar.		
The Civil War	Eli Whitney promotes the idea of mass producing guns by using interchangeable parts.		Abraham Lincoln is born on February 12, 1809, in Kentucky.	Military conflict between the North and South is narrowly averted as tension mounts over trade tariffs.
Canada			During the war of 1812, the British fight American militia forces at the Battle of Queenston Heights, and win.	Quebec City and Montreal are officially incorporated as cities.

Introduction

The United States of America grew from a young republic to a powerful nation during the 19th century. The Louisiana Purchase in 1803 nearly doubled the size of the country, and victories in wars against Britain, Spain, and Mexico gave the Americans control of lands from the Atlantic to the Pacific coasts. As the country and its economy developed, the rifts deepened between the North and South, resulting in the Civil War (1861–65). The century ended with major developments in business, technology, and transportation. In the north, Canada grew from a few colonies governed by the British to a nation that spanned the continent. Relations among its peoples, who included a large French population, were fairly peaceful, and by the end of the century self-rule was established. This book tells the story of the two expanding nations, including the triumphs and the human costs, particularly to the Native Americans, the African Americans, and the soldiers and families affected by the Civil War.

James Monroe (1758–1831) pledged that the Americas would "henceforth not to be considered as subjects for future colonization by any European Power."

William Clark's compass, carried on his famous expedition with Meriwether Lewis.

The North West Mounted Police wore striking red jackets and stetson-style hats.

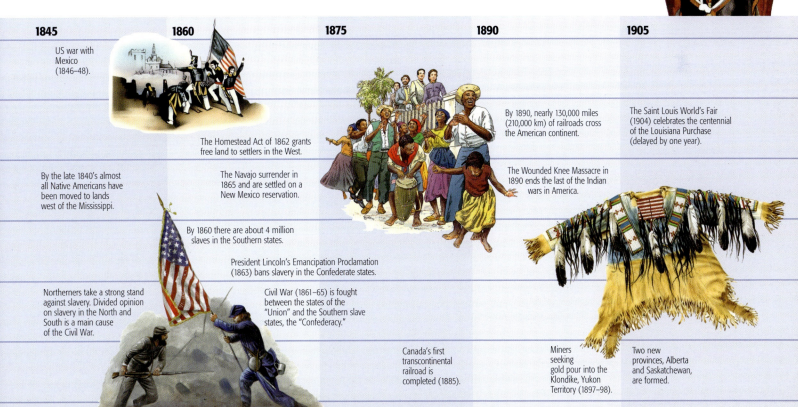

Plains Indians, who lived on the Great Plains in the central part of North America, wore clothing and moccasins made of animal skins. Each tribe had its own unique culture.

A family and their animals outside their house, made of mud and grass, in Kansas, in about 1860. Pioneers settled across the Great Plains during the 19th century.

Growth of a Modern Nation

The United States began as thirteen colonies on the east coast, but by the end of the 1800s the nation extended all the way to the west coast. The Native Americans were forced into increasingly smaller pockets of land as white settlers spread west. Towns and cities grew up across the continent, and millions of immigrants swelled the work force. By the end of the century, America was no longer an underpopulated agricultural nation, but a leading industrial one.

Native Peoples
Native American peoples had strong cultures and traditions that had developed over the centuries. In the 19th century, white settlers wanted to take their lands. The native people tried hard to hold on to their lands and ways of life. Some adopted European ways and tried to fit in; others fought back. But eventually the American government forced them to give up their homes and move to reservations on less desirable land.

Pioneers Push Back the Frontier
The century began with the expansionist policy of President Thomas Jefferson, who in 1803 bought the Louisiana Territory from France, nearly doubling the size of the United States. Settlers were encouraged to claim land across the country, often pushing out native peoples. To start with, the settlers only possessions were those they had brought with them. Wars against Britain, Spain, and Mexico resulted in American control of land across the continent.

Opening up the West
"Go west, young man, and grow up with the country," wrote an Indiana journalist in 1851, encouraging young men to take advantage of the opportunities of the American frontier. Many thousands of Americans heeded his advice. From the early 1840s, explorers, pioneers, immigrants, and gold seekers traveled west in search of adventure, land, wealth, religious freedom, and a new life. The American government supported them in an effort to gain control of more land.

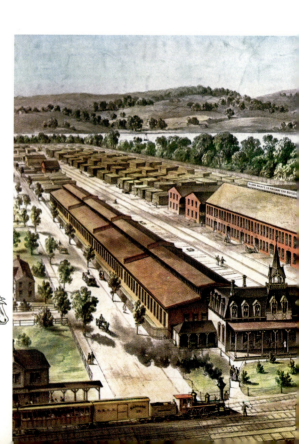

Pioneers traveled by covered wagon and stagecoach during the mid 1800s. By the end of the century most people traveled by train.

The Slavery Issue

Southerners relied on slaves for labor of all kinds, but especially for the hard work of planting and picking cotton, which was central to the Southern economy. By 1860 there were about 4 million slaves in the South. Northerners, who increasingly earned money through business and manufacturing, did not need slaves for their livelihood. Many of them were abolitionists, people who opposed slavery. They felt that slavery was cruel and violated the principal of freedom that was the basis of the US Constitution.

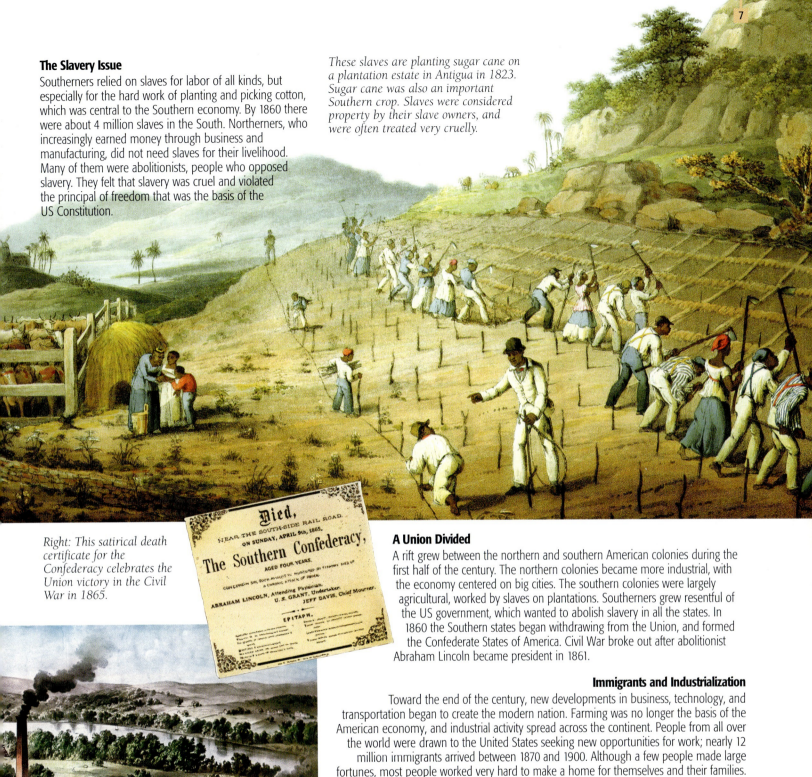

These slaves are planting sugar cane on a plantation estate in Antigua in 1823. Sugar cane was also an important Southern crop. Slaves were considered property by their slave owners, and were often treated very cruelly.

Right: This satirical death certificate for the Confederacy celebrates the Union victory in the Civil War in 1865.

A Union Divided

A rift grew between the northern and southern American colonies during the first half of the century. The northern colonies became more industrial, with the economy centered on big cities. The southern colonies were largely agricultural, worked by slaves on plantations. Southerners grew resentful of the US government, which wanted to abolish slavery in all the states. In 1860 the Southern states began withdrawing from the Union, and formed the Confederate States of America. Civil War broke out after abolitionist Abraham Lincoln became president in 1861.

Immigrants and Industrialization

Toward the end of the century, new developments in business, technology, and transportation began to create the modern nation. Farming was no longer the basis of the American economy, and industrial activity spread across the continent. People from all over the world were drawn to the United States seeking new opportunities for work; nearly 12 million immigrants arrived between 1870 and 1900. Although a few people made large fortunes, most people worked very hard to make a home for themselves and their families.

Left: The Wason Manufacturing Company, in Springfield, Massachusetts, made the railway carriages for the first transcontinental railway, completed in 1869.

Right: Jewish immigrants brought tailoring skills, among others, to the United States during the 19th century.

THE FRENCH AND BARBARY WARS

1797
The XYZ Affair sparks the Quasi War between the United States and France.

1798
Eli Whitney promotes the idea of mass producing guns by using interchangeable parts.

1800
The Convention of 1800 ends America's alliance with France, which has existed since 1778. The US seat of government moves from Philadelphia to Washington, D.C.

1801–09
Thomas Jefferson is third president of the United States.

1804
The Intrepid, under Stephen Decatur, successfully attacks Tripoli harbor, but later, rechristened as the fire ship Inferno and captained by Richard Somers, it explodes.

1808
The foreign slave trade is made illegal; prices for slaves soar.

The French and Barbary Wars

During the 1790s, the war between Britain and France gave America the opportunity to trade with both sides as a neutral country. Its exports soared. France, however, declared that it would seize any neutral ships carrying British goods. America was held to ransom; France would only agree to stop attacking US ships in return for money. America responded by capturing 85 French ships, although war was never officially declared. In the Mediterranean, US ships came under attack from North African Barbary pirates. The conflict lasted until 1805.

Mass-Produced Guns
Eli Whitney (1765–1825) was an inventor. He promoted the idea of using interchangeable parts to make guns. Until 1798, guns had been made by hand; if one part broke, a new part had to be specially made. Whitney used power machinery and unskilled workers to make gun parts using molds. The identical parts could be assembled quickly, and any part would fit any gun.

In 1798, in preparation for war with France, the US government gave Whitney a contract to make 10,000 muskets like this one.

The XYZ Affair and the Quasi War
French attacks on US ships carrying British goods caused tension to mount between the two nations. In 1797, US President John Adams sent some delegates to France to negotiate peace terms. The delegates met three French agents (later known as X, Y, and Z), who demanded money in return for letting the delegates meet the French foreign minister. America was furious, and naval battles between America and France ensued. The conflict—which became known as the "Quasi" War, because no official declaration of war was made—was resolved by a treaty in 1800.

Right: In 1785, Thomas Jefferson (1743–1826) was the US ambassador to France. He strongly objected to his government's policy of paying money to the pirates of North Africa to stop them attacking US ships. Jefferson was elected president in 1801.

After Jefferson ended the foreign slave trade, slaves continued to be sold within the USA at public auctions like this one.

Ban on the Foreign Slave Trade
Thomas Jefferson believed strongly in personal freedom and he condemned the slave trade, which he blamed on England's King George III. In 1807 Jefferson signed a bill prohibiting the importation of slaves. The ban took effect on 1 January, 1808. Estimates vary, but some suggest the United States imported as many as 170,000 slaves between 1783 and 1808.

Founding Father Alexander Hamilton, the first Secretary of the Treasury, was a major-general in the army during the Quasi War.

THE BARBARY WARS

The Barbary Coast
The Barbary Wars were fought in the Mediterranean Sea off the coast of North Africa. The region was also known as the Barbary Coast (Barbary is derived from "Berber," the name of the region's original inhabitants). The main ports used by the Barbary pirates were Tripoli (in Tripolitania, the northwest region of Libya), Algiers, Salé, and other ports in Morocco.

The Barbary Wars

From the 17th century, Barbary pirates in North Africa had been demanding money from Britain and France in exchange for the safe passage of their ships across the Mediterranean. After 1783, the newly independent America also had to start paying tribute to protect its ships. For 18 years it paid out huge sums. But during this time, America's naval strength was growing. In 1801 the new president, Thomas Jefferson, refused to pay any more money to the Barbary rulers. War broke out with Tripolitania and lasted until 1805, when a treaty was signed that stopped payments to Tripoli and ended the First Barbary War.

Stephen Decatur's Night Raid

Stephen Decatur (1779–1820) became a national hero during the Barbary Wars. In 1804 he led a daring night raid into Tripoli harbor, where the captured US warship *Philadelphia* was at anchor. Lieutenant Decatur managed to destroy the ship, preventing its use by the enemy. He was made a captain at the age of 25, and later led troops against the British in the War of 1812.

Decatur's ship, the Intrepid, disguised to look like a Barbary ship, successfully sets fire to the USS Philadelphia in Tripoli harbor, February 1804.

THE LOUISIANA PURCHASE

America Doubles in Size
President Thomas Jefferson's government bought the Louisiana Territory for about $15 million. The vast area covered more than 800,000 square miles (2 million sq km), and stretched from the Mississippi River west to the Rocky Mountains, and from the Gulf of Mexico north all the way to the border with Canada.

The French flag is lowered and the American flag raised in New Orleans' town square to mark the Louisiana Purchase in 1803.

A statue of Lewis and Clark was erected in Oregon, at the end of their trail to the West Coast. Clark wrote in his journal, "Ocean in view! O! the joy."

LEWIS AND CLARK

1803
The United States buys the Louisiana Territory from France.

1804
Lewis and Clark set off on their expedition in May. In November, French Canadian fur trader Toussaint Charbonneau and his Shoshone Indian wife Sacagawea are hired as interpreters and guides.

1805
The expedition reaches the West Coast in November.

1806
The return journey begins in March. In July the group divides up to find shorter routes and explore more territory. The members of the expedition reunite in September and return to St. Louis.

Lewis and Clark

In 1803 the United States bought a huge area of land, the Louisiana Territory, from France. This largely uncharted territory needed exploring. Led by US army captain Meriwether Lewis and lieutenant William Clark, a group of nearly 50 men set out in May 1804 on a journey of discovery that took more than two years. Starting near St. Louis, Missouri, they covered about 8,000 miles (12,800 km), traveling by boat, horse, and on foot all the way to the West Coast and back again. On the way they mapped the region and recorded valuable information about the native peoples, animals and plants.

The Expedition
The explorers, called "the Corps of Discovery," started their journey aboard a 55-foot (17-m) long keelboat, which they took up the Missouri River. The men kept detailed journals, and Lewis identified 178 new plant species and 122 animals. Although they had to navigate dangerous rivers, cross mountains, and face wild animals, as well as extreme hunger and cold, only one man died on the journey.

Right: Clark's notebook contained a sketch of the expedition's keelboat. His notes, and particularly his maps, provided valuable information about the northwest region of America.

William Clark's compass was one of many instruments carried by the expedition.

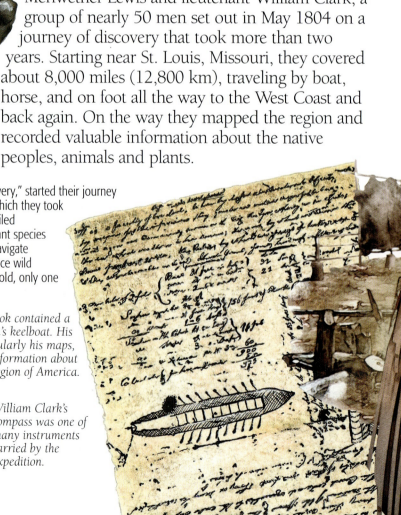

THE ROUTE

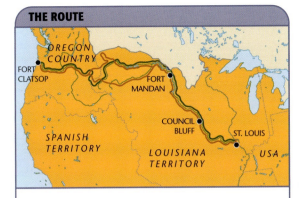

Following the Rivers
One purpose of the expedition was to find a river route across the northwest, for commercial reasons. After following the Missouri up river, Lewis and Clark crossed the Rocky Mountains and then followed the Clearwater, Snake, and Columbia rivers, which took them to the Pacific Ocean.

Outward journey — Return journey and explorations

Fort Clatsop

The expedition built Fort Clatsop in what is now northern Oregon, in December, 1805. Finished on Christmas Day, it was their last camp before their return journey. They spent a wet and cold winter there before heading back up the Columbia River in March, 1806.

Lewis and Clark named their 1805–06 winter quarters Fort Clatsop, after the friendly Native Americans who lived in the region. This replica was built in the 1950s.

Sacagawea was born a Shoshone Indian, but was kidnapped as a girl by the Hidatsa Indians, so she spoke both languages. The expedition took her along as an interpreter. When they reached her Shoshone tribe, the chief turned out to be her long-lost brother. Sacagawea helped the expedition obtain horses from the Shoshone for crossing the mountains. Her baby son, Jean-Baptiste, was nicknamed "Pomp" by Clark.

The War of 1812

Relations were tense between the United States and Britain in the early 1800s. Britain's tight control on shipping—a consequence of the war between Britain and France—affected American trade. Britain also caused bitterness by stopping US merchant ships and searching them for British naval deserters. Thousands of suspected deserters were "pressed," or forced, into British service. Meanwhile, disputes continued over the border with Canada, where Britain was giving military aid to the Shawnee people to help them defend their lands from American settlers. War with Britain broke out in 1812 and ended in 1814, with no clear victor.

The Battle of Tippecanoe
In 1811, General William Henry Harrison, governor of the Indiana Territory in the northwest of the United States, was intent on clearing the Shawnee people from the region so that American settlers could take over the land. Two Shawnee brothers, Tecumseh (see page 15) and Tenskwatawa, led a confederacy of tribes to resist the settlers. Harrison and the Shawnee came to blows at the Battle of Tippecanoe, in Indiana. Harrison's army fought off a Shawnee attack and burned their village.

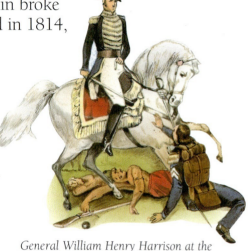

General William Henry Harrison at the Battle of Tippecanoe. Although many of his men were killed, the battle was considered a US victory.

Naval Encounters in the Atlantic
The British had a much larger and more powerful navy than the United States at this time, but the Americans won some significant naval victories during the war. Only weeks after war was declared, the USS *Constitution* captured and burned HMS *Guerrière*. By June 1813, the British blockade of US ports was so tight that most US ships were unable to leave harbor. The USS *Chesapeake*, commanded by Captain James Lawrence, defied the blockade and engaged HMS *Shannon* off Boston harbor. The British won a fierce battle and captured the *Chesapeake*.

Captain James Lawrence (1781–1813) was mortally wounded defending the Chesapeake. His dying words, "Don't give up the ship," became legendary.

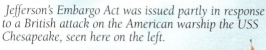

Jefferson's Embargo Act was issued partly in response to a British attack on the American warship the USS Chesapeake, seen here on the left.

The Embargo Act of 1807
In an effort to prevent the British and French from interfering with US shipping, the US Congress passed the Embargo Act of 1807. The act made it illegal for American ships carrying export goods to land in any foreign port. It also set strict rules limiting British imports. The aim was to hurt Britain, which would lose food and supplies. But it was US farmers, who could no longer sell their produce, who were hit hardest. The act was later repealed.

The Battle of Queenston Heights
On June 18, 1812, the Americans declared war on the British. One of their aims was to drive the British out of Canada. In October 1812, a large American force crossed the Niagara River into Canada. For a while they held their position, but lacking reinforcements, they were surrounded and captured near the town of Queenston. The British commander, Major General Sir Isaac Brock—known as the "Hero of Upper Canada"—died in the battle.

THE WAR OF 1812

THE NORTHERN FRONTIER

US Invasion Plans
At the outbreak of the war, in 1812, the US army planned to march into the British colonies of Upper Canada (present-day southern Ontario) and Lower Canada (present-day Québec) and take control. They planned to invade at four strategic points: across from Detroit, in the Niagara area, at Kingston, and south of Montréal. From there they planned to march on and capture Québec City. Both sides won and lost some significant battles, but in the end the British held on to their colonies.

Laura Ingersoll Secord and the Battle of Beaverdams
After crossing into Canada, the US army occupied the Niagara Peninsula. Some of the officers took over the house of James and Laura Secord, and used it as their headquarters to plan an attack on the local Canadian militia, commanded by Lieutenant James FitzGibbon. Laura overheard their plans, and bravely walked 20 miles (32 km) across dangerous territory to warn FitzGibbon. Prepared for the attack, the militia and their Native American allies were able to defeat the Americans at the Battle of Beaverdams, on June 24, 1813.

Laura Ingersoll Secord (1775–1868) and her homestead in Queenston, Ontario. She kept quiet about what she had done and survived the war to live to an old age.

Sir Isaac Brock (1769–1812) was mortally wounded at the Battle of Queenston Heights. His final words were reported to be: "Push on, brave York Volunteers."

THE WAR OF 1812

1812
In August, Native Americans under Shawnee leader Tecumseh help the British capture Detroit. In October, the British win the Battle of Queenston Heights in Canada.

1813
In April, US forces capture York (now Toronto) in Upper Canada. More victories follow in September, when US forces led by Captain Oliver Perry win the Battle of Lake Erie, and in October, when US forces win the Battle of the Thames in Canada. Tecumseh is killed, and this leads to the collapse of the Native American Confederation.

1814
In August, British troops invade Washington, D.C., and burn the White House. They attack Fort McHenry in Baltimore in September, inspiring Francis Scott Key to write "The Star-Spangled Banner" (which Congress names the American National Anthem in 1931). The Treaty of Ghent officially ends the war on Christmas Eve.

1815
In January, US forces win the Battle of New Orleans, before hearing that the war is over.

An engraving by George Catlin (1796–1872) showing the Choctaw Ball-Play Dance. This ceremonial dance would take place before a game of stickball was played. Stickball later developed into the sport of lacrosse.

THE FIVE TRIBES

1809–21
Sequoyah develops his system for writing the Cherokee language.

1811–12
The New Madrid earthquakes rock Creek lands in Louisiana Territory (now Missouri). Many Creeks believe these earthquakes are an omen.

1813
The Battle of Burnt Corn, in what is now Alabama, brings the United States into the Creek War. Tecumseh's death in the War of 1812 marks the end of his Native American Confederation and any strong resistance to white settlement.

1814
By the Treaty of Fort Jackson, after the Battle of Horseshoe Bend, the Creeks are forced to cede some 23 million acres (93,000 sq km) of land to the United States.

1828
The Cherokee Phoenix, the first Native American newspaper, is launched.

1830
The US Congress passes the Indian Removal Act, which forces most of the five tribes to move to the Oklahoma Territory.

The Five Tribes

In the years following the American War of Independence, tension grew between white settlers and Native Americans over land ownership. The southeast was home to five large tribes: the Cherokee, Chickasaw, Choctaw, Creek, and Seminole peoples. Each tribe had its own towns and schools. When white settlers began claiming their land, the native peoples tried many things to keep their homes, including adopting European ways. The US government, however, forced almost all of them to move to a designated region called the Oklahoma Territory.

The Five "Civilized" Tribes

Europeans called the peoples of the southeast the five "civilized" tribes, because many of them adopted European styles of dress, farming, and education. The Seminole people (an offshoot of the Creeks) moved south to Florida and accepted other people, including runaway slaves, into their tribe. The Chickasaw and Choctaw languages, like the Seminole and Creek, are Muskogean, while the Cherokee language is Iroquoian.

Creek Way of Life

Creek towns consisted of mud houses with thatched roofs, surrounding a central plaza used for meetings and ceremonies. Sometimes the towns had a dome-shaped temple built on top of an earth mound. Creek women were mostly responsible for the farms, where they grew maize, beans, and squash. They also kept livestock and gathered wild plants. The men were hunters, fishermen, and warriors.

The Creek War

The Creek War started as a civil war between the Creek Indians. A group of Creek warriors called the "Red Sticks," after their red war clubs, clashed with other Creek chiefs over the encroachment by whites onto their land. They also attacked Creeks who had adopted white ways. In 1813, the US army was drawn into the conflict when a group of soldiers looted some Creek munitions that had been bought with British money. Various attacks followed, including the massacre of several hundred people at Fort Mims in Alabama by the Red Sticks. US troops retaliated at the Battle of Horseshoe Bend, where the Red Sticks were crushed in 1814.

Creek "Red Stick" chief William Weatherford (1780–1824), or "Red Eagle", surrendered to US general Andrew Jackson after the Battle of Horseshoe Bend. Jackson released him on the condition that he keep the peace.

THE FIVE TRIBES 15

Opposition to White Expansion

The Shawnee chief Tecumseh (see page 12) was the inspirational leader of Native American resistance to white encroachment at this time. Tecumseh believed that the only way to combat the threat was for all Native Americans to unite as a single political body, rather than as a loose confederation. In 1812, he visited the Five Tribes of the southeast on a mission to recruit allies. Although many of the southern nations rejected his appeals, he gained the support of the Creek "Red Sticks."

In this drawing, Chief Tecumseh (1768–1813) is shown wearing a British tunic and medal—a sign of his allegiance to Britain and opposition to the United States.

The Cherokee Language

Cherokee was only a spoken language until a Cherokee Indian named Sequoyah invented the written language. During the Creek War, Sequoyah realized how significant it was that he and his people could not write letters home, read military orders, or keep a diary of events. So after the war, he made up 86 different symbols to represent the sounds made in speech. Using this system, the Cherokee people were able to read and write in Cherokee, and books and newspapers could be published.

An illustration of the Cherokee writing system. Sequoyah (c.1770–1843), also known as George Guess, called his Cherokee language symbols "talking leaves."

Many southeastern tribes held an annual pre-harvest Green Corn festival, celebrating rebirth, thanksgiving, and forgiveness. People would clean and rebuild their villages, pray, fast, dance, and feast.

Texas and Mexico

In 1820, the United States stretched from the east coast westward only as far as present-day Louisiana. The whole of the southwest, including Mexico and Texas, was part of Spain's colonial empire. American settlers were not content with this. They wanted to own all the land between the Atlantic and the Pacific Oceans. Texan independence and victory in the war against Mexico added more than 500,000 sq miles (1,300,000 sq km) of land to the United States.

The Monroe Doctrine
In 1823, President James Monroe gave a famous speech outlining his foreign policy. He pledged that the United States would not interfere in any wars within Europe. He also said that he would not tolerate attempts by European powers to colonize any part of the Americas. Monroe adopted this policy, which later became known as the "Monroe Doctrine," partly because he was worried that Spain might try to reclaim some of its colonies (Argentina, Chile, and Peru, for example) in South America.

James Monroe (1758–1831) pledged that the Americas would "henceforth not to be considered as subjects for future colonization by any European Power."

Missions in Texas
Spanish Catholic missionaries were sent to Texas not just to convert the Native Americans to Christianity, but also to teach them Spanish ways of living and Spanish politics, and to integrate them into the Spanish empire. The missions were institutions, protected and controlled by the Spanish state—some had soldiers posted at them. Missionaries tried to oversee almost every aspect of the Native Americans' daily life, including work, prayer, and leisure activities. Many native peoples resisted their rigid ideals. There were 27 missions in Texas operating from the late 1600s to the early 1800s.

The San Jose mission in San Antonio, Texas, was completed in 1782. The church doorway is surrounded by typical Spanish baroque decoration.

Mexico Gains Independence from Spain
In 1810, in the small town of Dolores in central Mexico, the parish priest, Miguel Hidalgo y Costilla (1753–1811), joined a group of patriots and began promoting the idea of Mexican independence. Many native Mexicans were angry that they were so poor compared to their Spanish rulers. The uprising that Hidalgo and his patriot friends started developed into a war of independence that was to last more than 10 years. During the last year of the war, in 1821, Spanish army leader Agustin de Iturbide (1783–1824) changed sides, allying himself with the rebels against the Spanish government. The Spanish were defeated and Mexico gained its independence.

Agustin de Iturbide was a lieutenant in the Spanish army before joining the rebels. As Agustin I, he was emperor (1822–23) of the newly independent Mexico.

Texas Gains Independence from Mexico
In 1821, an American named Stephen Austin (1793–1836) gained permission from the newly formed Mexican government to establish an American colony in Texas (then a province of Mexico). Settlers were given land on condition that they became Mexican citizens and Catholics. Soon the settlers outnumbered the Mexicans, and they demanded independence from Mexico's oppressive regime. War broke out in 1835. The following year, Sam Houston (1793–1863), commander-in-chief of the Texan army, led his troops in a surprise attack on Mexican dictator Santa Anna's army. The Texans won the war and gained independence for Texas.

The "Lone Star" flag became Texas's national flag in 1839 and then its state flag when it joined the union in 1845.

Remember the Alamo!
The siege of the Alamo is one of the most legendary battles in American history. A force of 3,000 Mexican troops led by Santa Anna marched on San Antonio in 1836. There they were met by only 187 American men, defending themselves inside a mission called the Alamo. The Americans succeeded in holding the Alamo for 10 days, killing about half of the Mexicans, but eventually they were all killed. The following month, "Remember the Alamo!" became the American war cry at the battle of San Jacinto, the last battle in the war that won Texas its independence.

The Mexican War of 1846

Having gained its independence from Mexico, Texas remained independent for nine years. Then, in 1845, it was allowed to join the United States as the 28th state. Mexico, still bitter at having lost Texas and unwilling to relinquish its claim on the province, felt provoked by the annexation into attacking American soldiers on Texas's southern border. War broke out in 1846, and was won by the United States in 1848. As a result, the USA gained what are now the states of New Mexico, Arizona, Utah, Nevada, and California.

US forces under General Winfield Scott (1786–1866) captured Mexico City on September 13, 1847, effectively winning the Mexican War.

The Siege of the Alamo made heroes of Colonel William B. Travis (1808–1836) and frontiersmen Jim Bowie (1796–1836) and Davy Crockett (1786–1836). Crockett became a legendary folk hero in America.

TEXAS AND MEXICO

1819
By the Adams-Onís Treaty, Spain cedes Florida to the USA and the USA renounces claims to Texas. (The treaty takes effect in 1821).

1821
Agustin de Iturbide and rebel leader Vicente Guerrero declare Mexican independence.

1836
After a final, victorious battle, Sam Houston (wounded with a bullet in his leg) secures Texas's independence.

1846
The United States declares war on Mexico. US forces under General Zachary Taylor capture Monterrey, Mexico.

1847
US forces under General Winfield Scott capture Veracruz before traveling inland to take control of Mexico City.

1848
By the Treaty of Guadalupe Hidalgo, the Mexican War is ended.

The Trail of Tears

In the early 1800s it seemed nothing would stop the United States from expanding its territory. Native Americans already living in the United States were forced north and west by the American settlers. In the northeast, many of the Iroquois people moved north to Canada. In the southeast, the five tribes (see pages 14–15) were relocated to "Indian Territory" in what is now Oklahoma. The Cherokee people of northwestern Georgia were among the last to go, and their journey across the Midwest to Oklahoma became known as the Trail of Tears.

To celebrate the harvest, the Iroquois wore masks made of corn.

INDIAN REMOVAL

1829
Gold is discovered on Cherokee lands in northwestern Georgia.

1830
The Indian Removal Act allows the US government to move Native Americans west in exchange for their lands in the east.

1832
The Supreme Court rules that the Cherokee have a right to their land, but the federal government refuses to enforce it.

1835
A small faction of Cherokee sign the Treaty of New Echota, agreeing to move. The Cherokee majority under Chief John Ross (1790–1866) protest, but the treaty is enforced by the Supreme Court.

1835–42
In the second Seminole War, the Seminole people fight alongside runaway slaves against US troops to keep their land in Florida.

1838–39
Martin van Buren, US president 1837–41, oversees the removal of Cherokees along the Trail of Tears.

Around 14,000 Cherokee were forcibly moved from Georgia to "Indian Territory" in Oklahoma. The name "Trail of Tears" comes from the Cherokee Nunna-da-ul-tsun-yi, which means "the place where they cried."

Removal of the Cherokee

For many years the Cherokee lived among the white settlers in Georgia. They adopted European style government, schools, churches, and even wore colonial dress. But the US government was determined to remove them. Most Cherokee refused go, so in 1838 the government sent 7,000 soldiers to force them out. They were taken from their homes, at gunpoint if they resisted, and rounded up into camps. The 1,000 mile (1,600 km) journey to Oklahoma took four months, and thousands of Cherokee people died of cold, illness, and starvation on the way. When they finally arrived, they were confronted by more angry settlers who did not want them there.

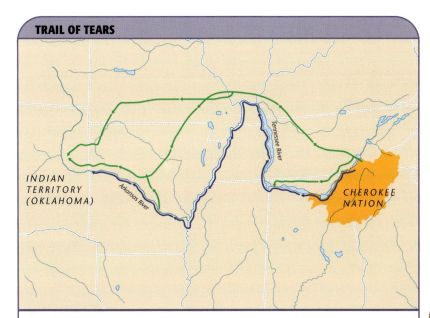

Two Routes Taken
The Cherokee were sent by one of two routes to Oklahoma. Some left Georgia on foot and horseback, traveling through Tennessee, Kentucky, Illinois, Missouri, and Arkansas before reaching Oklahoma. Others traveled by boat on the Tennessee, Ohio, Mississippi, and Arkansas rivers. Exhausted and sick people were not allowed to stop and rest during the journey, and many died.

- Cherokee Nation
- Overland route
- Water route

Removal Policy
In 1830, President Andrew Jackson signed the Indian Removal Act into law. It had been fiercely debated by Congress. Jackson believed that the Native Americans could never live peacefully among whites, and argued that moving them was in their best interests. Many Americans argued that the policy was unjust, immoral, and cruel.

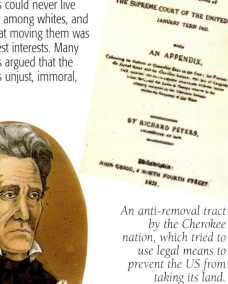

An anti-removal tract by the Cherokee nation, which tried to use legal means to prevent the US from taking its land.

Andrew Jackson (1767–1845), 7th US president, was a leading advocate of the removal of Native Americans.

Escaping Religious Persecution
The Mormons were another group who moved west during the mid 1800s. Facing religious persecution in Illinois, they began moving west in 1847. Led by Brigham Young (1801–77), they traveled to the Great Salt Lake Valley in what is now Utah. There they defended their right to practise their faith, and developed a strong community.

Mormons are members of the Church of Jesus Christ of Latter-Day Saints. The group's founder, Joseph Smith (1805–44) reported receiving golden plates from the angel Moroni, which he translated for publication as the Book of Mormon in 1830.

Gold and the Oregon Trail

During the mid 1800s, large numbers of Americans moved west. Pioneers, anxious to start a new life, were lured by reports from fur traders of fertile lands beyond the Rocky Mountains. The settlers traveled in covered wagons or by stagecoach along the Oregon Trail. Some 1,000 people joined missionary Marcus Whitman in the "great migration" in 1843. Then, in the late 1840s, gold seekers headed to California, hoping to make their fortune.

Above: San Francisco became a thriving city after the discovery of gold in 1849. This view overlooks the city from Telegraph Hill in 1850.

James Marshall's discovery of gold nuggets brought tens of thousands of "forty-niners" to California.

San Francisco
In the early 1840s, fewer than 50 people lived in the little hamlet of Yerba Buena, renamed San Francisco in 1847. With the discovery of gold, the town became the major supply center for miners. Its population rose from around 800 in 1848 to 25,000 in 1849, and in 1850 the town officially became a city. As people scrambled to get rich, business boomed, but so did violent crime. San Francisco continued to grow, and by 1870 had a population of nearly 150,000.

Panning involved swirling the gravel sediment from the riverbank around in a pan with some water. The gold flakes (or occasionally nuggets) would sink to the bottom of the pan.

The Discovery of Gold
John Sutter was an early trader living in the Sacramento Valley in California. He hired James W. Marshall, a carpenter, to help him build a mill. There, at the site of the mill, Marshall found some gold nuggets in 1848. Sutter and Marshall became business partners and tried to keep their discovery a secret, but word soon got out, and the following year thousands of people from all over the world traveled to California in search of gold. They were called "Forty-Niners," because they were part of the gold rush of 1849.

Panning for Gold
Miners spent long, gruelling days panning for gold. Food and supplies were expensive and hard to get. After the earliest gold finds, prospectors turned to placer mining to gather less easily accessible gold.

A poster advertising passage to the gold region of California aboard the clipper ship Josephine.

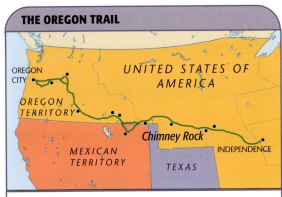

Along the Route
One of the main starting points for the Oregon Trail was Independence, Missouri, where travelers would load up their wagons with supplies. The route passed through many towns that had grown up around forts, such as Fort Laramie. Some people, exhausted by the journey, settled in these towns. Short-cuts and alternate routes, called "cutoffs," were made to bypass difficult terrain.

Wells Fargo stagecoaches carried passengers, freight, and mail, as well as gold and silver from the mines.

Stagecoaches and the Pony Express
Before the railways were built, stagecoaches carried mail, supplies, and passengers across often dangerous country to the next town. The largest stagecoach company was Wells Fargo, founded in 1852 to carry gold and provide banking services. In 1857, the Butterfield Overland Mail Company began a twice-weekly postal service between St. Louis, Missouri, and San Francisco. The journey took about 25 days. Faster than stagecoaches was the Pony Express. Men on horseback would carry the mail a certain distance, and then pass it to the next rider along the way, like a relay race.

From 1860 to 1861, horseback riders carried letters from Missouri to San Francisco in only 10 days by Pony Express.

The Oregon Trail
From the early 1840s, explorers, pioneers, and gold seekers used the Oregon Trail to travel west by covered wagon across America. The trail stretched from Independence, Missouri, for 2,000 miles (3,200 km) to the Columbia River in Oregon. Travelers undertook the six-month journey because they wanted land, wealth, adventure, or religious freedom. They often had to endure hunger, exhaustion, Native American attacks, extreme weather, floods, and diseases such as cholera. Travel on the Oregon Trail only declined in the late 1800s after trains replaced wagons for long journeys.

One of the landmarks for the early immigrants on the Oregon Trail was Chimney Rock, in what is now Nebraska.

White Southerners

The period of Southern history before the Civil War is often referred to as "antebellum" (from the Latin for "before the war"). Some people have a romantic view of this time; Margaret Mitchell's 1936 novel *Gone with the Wind* depicted the grand plantations and genteel living, and reached a wide audience. It was indeed a time of great prosperity for the large plantation owners, who grew rich from cotton, tobacco, and sugar cane. But their society was underpinned by slavery—a cause of growing tension with the North.

A master and slave at Legree Plantation, Capers Island, South Carolina. Plantation houses often had wide verandas and shuttered windows for shade.

Southern Whites dressed up to go out. Women carried parasols, as a suntan was considered unattractive.

Plantation House Architecture

During the first half of the 1800s, a type of neo-classical architecture called the Greek Revival style was very popular in the South. All types of buildings, including many plantation houses, were designed with white columns and grand porches like those of Greek temples. Some, such as Madewood Plantation House, built in 1848 in Napoleonville, Louisiana, were modelled on the Parthenon in Athens. Many buildings in Washington, D.C., such as the US Capitol, were also built in this style.

The Importance of Cotton

Following Eli Whitney's invention in 1793 of the cotton gin—a machine that separated cotton fiber from the seed pods—cotton became the main cash crop in the South. The plantations were worked by slaves (see pages 24–25), who did all the hard labor of picking, ginning, and baling the cotton. Plantation owners sometimes had several properties, and left the daily running of the plantation to an overseer. By 1850, the cotton industry had become vital to the economy of the South. Its importance was summed up in 1858 by senator James H. Hammond, who declared: "Cotton is king."

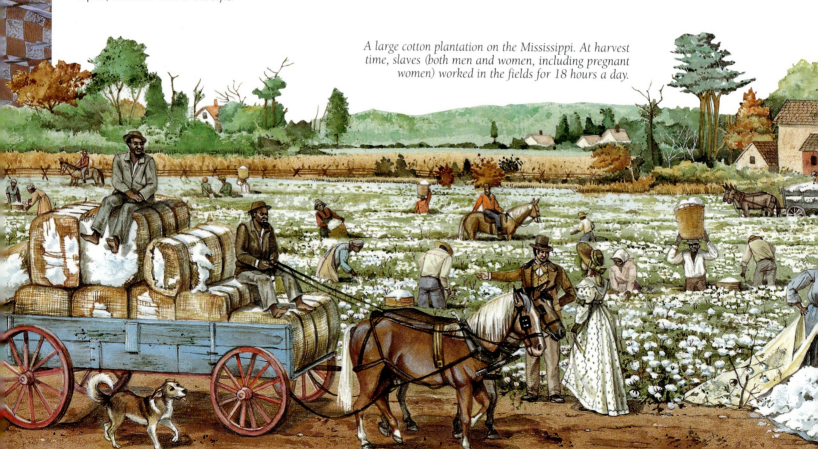

A large cotton plantation on the Mississippi. At harvest time, slaves (both men and women, including pregnant women) worked in the fields for 18 hours a day.

WHITE SOUTHERNERS

Steamboats
Steamboats were an important means of transportation for people in the South. The first steamboat on the Mississippi was the *New Orleans*, built in 1811. The following year, a regular steamboat service operated between New Orleans and Natchez, a distance of 268 miles (431 km). In 1816, improved designs meant that the boats could travel in shallower water. By 1830 there were 200 steamboats on the Mississippi carrying passengers and cargo.

Steamboats were driven by large paddlewheels. The fanciest boats had ornately decorated cabins, restaurants, and live music.

Defending Slavery
Some influential southern politicians passionately defended slavery. Senior politician John C. Calhoun (vice president 1825–32) argued that slavery was a "positive good" rather than a necessary evil. In a speech he made in 1837, he said that whites were naturally the dominant race and deserved to have slaves, and also that American slaves were treated better than slaves in other countries. Calhoun's views angered the many Northerners who opposed slavery. Such divisive sentiments became one of the main causes of the Civil War (see pages 28–31).

John C. Calhoun (1782–1850), from South Carolina, argued that slavery was good for both blacks and whites.

Sugar cane was crushed and refined in mills to make molasses, rum and fuel.

Sugar Plantations
In the early 1800s, some Southern planters began growing sugar cane, initially brought to America by Spanish explorers. It was a profitable crop, but required large amounts of land and heavy investment in machinery and slaves. Sugar plantations were especially common in Louisiana, where New Orleans plantation owner Etienne de Bore (1741–1820) developed the process of turning sugar into grains.

THE SOUTH

From 1800
Raised banks called levees are built along both banks of the Mississippi north of New Orleans to safeguard the land from flooding.

1816
Henry Miller Shreve launches his steamboat *Washington*, which travels from New Orleans, Louisiana, to Louisville, Kentucky.

1828
Congress passes the so-called Tariff of Abominations, which puts a high tax on imported goods. Britain, in response, imports less cotton from the Southern states, damaging their economy.

1832
South Carolina declares the 1828 tariffs to be unconstitutional, because they favor Northern manufacturing over Southern agriculture. Military conflict between the North and South is narrowly averted by the introduction of a compromise tariff in 1833.

1843
Norbert Rillieux (1806–1894) invents an evaporator pan system to separate sugar from sugar cane.

1854
The Kansas–Nebraska Act opens up the Midwest to settlement. Settlers there can choose whether or not to allow slavery.

Slavery and the Underground Railroad

Slaves were owned by many early Americans, particularly plantation owners in the South, who needed lots of workers to provide labor. Although abolitionists—people who opposed slavery—helped pass laws during the 1800s to restrict slavery, by 1860 there were about four million slaves in the South. Slaves were considered property and were often separated from their families and forced to work under very harsh conditions. Many tried to run away, and some succeeded, using a secret network of routes called the Underground Railroad.

Hitching posts like this black lawn jockey signalled a safe house to slaves using the Underground Railroad.

SLAVERY

1793
Eli Whitney's invention of the cotton gin makes separating cotton from its seeds quicker and easier. More slaves are needed on plantations. Cotton becomes an important crop for the Southern economy.

1821
The US government passes The Missouri Compromise, admitting Missouri as a slave state and Maine as a free state, and prohibiting slavery in most of the western territory.

c.1830
Runaway slaves first use the Underground Railroad to reach freedom.

1849
Harriet Tubman makes her first rescue on the Underground Railroad.

1850
The Fugitive Slave Law is made much harsher. Slave owners are allowed to hunt for runaways anywhere in the country. People who help them, even in free states, may be punished. Slaves are not allowed to have a trial in court.

1854
The Kansas-Nebraska Act reverses the Missouri Compromise, allowing slavery in those territories.

Slave Markets
Most slave families in the United States came originally from Africa. They were brought by ships, in which they were forced to live below deck in crowded, filthy conditions. Many died on the journey. When they arrived, they were sold at markets or at auctions to the highest bidders. The children of slaves were considered slaves too, and were sold in the same way. Potential owners would choose slaves just as they would choose new animals, looking at their muscles, teeth, and other physical attributes to make sure they were strong and would make good workers.

Slave auctions, watched by white citizens, were humiliating and terrifying for the slaves. Once sold, they had to go wherever their new owner took them.

PRE-CIVIL WAR SLAVE AND FREE STATES

- Slave states
- Territory open to slavery
- Free states and territories

Underground Railroad Lines
Routes, or "lines," on the Underground Railroad covered hundreds of miles. They mostly ran from the slave states in the South northward to free states, such as Pennsylvania. Some ran southward through Florida to the Caribbean islands. Runaways traveling north were advised to follow the North Star. Some of the routes to Canada involved crossing Lake Erie. For part of the year it was possible to cross the lake by boat, but in winter ice floes barred the way, and some slaves tried to cross the ice on foot.

Helped by "Moses"

Harriet "Moses" Tubman was born a slave in Maryland. In 1849 she escaped to the city of Philadelphia in Pennsylvania, which was a free state. There, she vowed to return to Maryland to help other slaves escape to freedom. Although the Fugitive Slave Law of 1850 made it a crime to help a runaway slave, "Moses" made 19 rescue trips and helped more than 300 slaves find freedom using the Underground Railroad.

Harriet Tubman (c.1820–1913) was called "Moses" after the Biblical prophet who led the Jewish people to freedom from Egypt.

Slaves on Cotton Plantations

Cotton became a very important crop in the South, and plantation owners used slaves for the hard work of planting and picking it. Field hands usually lived in very basic huts and supplemented their rations with food they grew in their gardens. The combination of relentless, backbreaking work and poor living conditions left them vulnerable to many diseases. They were constantly threatened with violent punishments or sale to another plantation, which would separate them from family and friends.

A slave family on a cotton plantation in Georgia, in about 1860. Even young children were put to work in the fields.

The Underground Railroad

The Underground Railroad was a network of escape routes taken by runaway slaves seeking freedom. Along each route, the slaves were helped by sympathetic people who opposed slavery. Often at great personal risk, they would break the law by providing the slaves with food, clothing, shelter, and directions to free (non-slave) states or Canada. Escaping slaves used a secret code that drew on railway terminology (hence the name "Underground Railroad"). For example, the people who helped the slaves were called "conductors," the safe houses were "stations," and the routes taken were "lines." Even after gaining freedom, slaves still faced poverty and discrimination, as well as the constant threat of being captured and returned to slavery in the South.

Below: Runaway slaves often traveled at night along rivers and creeks, because there was less traffic on the rivers, and so less chance of being seen. Bounty hunters, who were paid for capturing runaway slaves, pursued the fugitives with bloodhounds.

The North: Factories and Cities

This engraving from about 1819 shows women working in a textile mill. Some factories, such as those of Francis Cabot Lowell, were initially known for their good working conditions.

Growth of Textile Mills
In New England in the northeast, textile mills were built for turning raw cotton, bought from the Southern plantations, into cloth. Knowledge of the machinery needed to spin and weave was brought from England by American merchant Francis Cabot Lowell (1775–1817). He improved the machinery and brought all the tasks under one roof. Mill towns for the workers grew up around the booming industry.

THE NORTH: FACTORIES AND CITIES

1813
Francis Cabot Lowell forms the Boston Manufacturing Company and in 1814 sets up a cotton factory at Waltham, Massachusetts. Although Lowell dies in 1817, his memory lives on in the new mill town of Lowell, Mass., founded in 1822.

1817
Construction of the Erie Canal begins.

1833
William Lloyd Garrison (1805–79) founds the American Anti-Slavery Society.

1846
Elias Howe (1819–67) invents the first sewing machine.

1848
The first US convention for women's rights is held; Elizabeth Cady Stanton reads the Declaration of Sentiments, calling for equal rights for women.

1850
The Fugitive Slave Law makes Northern officials responsible for enforcing slavery, fuelling the abolitionist movement.

1851–52
Harriet Beecher Stowe's Uncle Tom's Cabin is first published in serial form.

"Safe lifts" were first used by the public in 1857, in a tall New York department store.

The Seneca Falls Convention
The summer of 1848 was an exciting time for women's rights supporters. The first women's rights convention was held in July in Seneca Falls, New York. It was organized by abolitionists Elizabeth Cady Stanton (1815–1902) and Lucretia Coffin Mott (1793–1880). About 300 people attended. Stanton later worked with civil rights leader Susan B. Anthony (1820–1906) to gain the vote for women.

Lucretia Coffin Mott, shown here in 1878, was considered one of the first American feminists.

Northern Cities Expand Upwards
New businesses brought more people to the cities in the mid 1800s. In cities like New York, there was little space to build but upwards. Taller buildings were built, using new innovations and cheaper materials. Innovations included the first "safe lift," designed by Elisha Otis (1811–61); the lift incorporated a safety device that prevented it from falling if the cable broke.

The Erie Canal
New York City is built at the mouth of the Hudson River. When the Erie Canal was completed in 1825, it linked the Hudson River (and thus New York) to Lake Erie to the west. Settlers were able to travel from the city all the way to the Great Lakes first by river and then by canal, and trade opened up in both directions. Before long New York became the center of commerce in the United States.

L ife in the North and South became increasingly different as the century wore on. In the early 1800s, most people in both regions were farmers, but before long manufacturing and industry became more important in the North. Cities expanded, and many immigrants arrived looking for work. Religious and social reform groups flourished, supporting causes such as better education, women's rights, temperance (not drinking alcohol), and the abolition of slavery. Divided opinion in the North and South on slavery was a main cause of the Civil War.

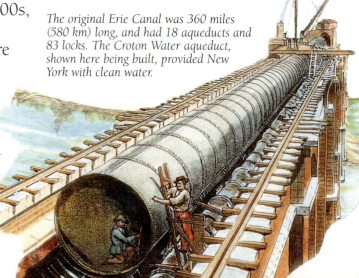

The original Erie Canal was 360 miles (580 km) long, and had 18 aqueducts and 83 locks. The Croton Water aqueduct, shown here being built, provided New York with clean water.

THE NORTH: FACTORIES AND CITIES 27

A poster advertising the anti-slavery novel Uncle Tom's Cabin, a best-seller in the 1800s.

Abolitionists
Northerners began to take a strong stand against slavery, and abolitionists came from many walks of life. William Lloyd Garrison's American Anti-Slavery Society demanded the immediate emancipation of slaves. The harsh Fugitive Slave Law of 1850 inspired Harriet Beecher Stowe (1811–96) to write her popular novel *Uncle Tom's Cabin* (1852), which exposed the inhumanity of slavery and further fuelled abolitionist passions.

Although thriving by the 1850s, New York City also suffered a series of economic crises. As this painting shows, in 1857 bankers on Wall Street panicked as grain prices dropped and businesses faced collapse.

New York City
By the mid 1800s, New York City had the advantage of good access to shipping, railroads, and canals, as well as a large number of people looking for work. American poet Walt Whitman described the bustle in New York as a "…ceaseless, devilish, provoking, delicious, glorious jam!"

Clothing Industry Revolutionized
Before the sewing machine was invented, people sewed clothing by hand at home, and clothes were expensive. The mass production of sewing machines in the 1850s meant that clothing, such as uniforms during the Civil War, could be manufactured cheaply in large quantities in factories. Isaac Singer (1811–75) achieved enduring success by designing a practical sewing machine that he marketed to housewives. Increasingly, however, Americans bought ready-made clothing.

A Singer sewing machine from the 1850s.

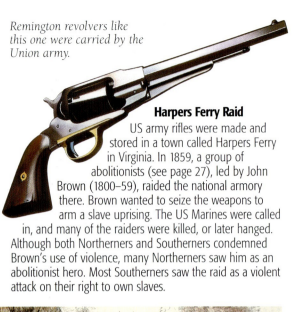

Remington revolvers like this one were carried by the Union army.

Harpers Ferry Raid

US army rifles were made and stored in a town called Harpers Ferry in Virginia. In 1859, a group of abolitionists (see page 27), led by John Brown (1800–59), raided the national armory there. Brown wanted to seize the weapons to arm a slave uprising. The US Marines were called in, and many of the raiders were killed, or later hanged. Although both Northerners and Southerners condemned Brown's use of violence, many Northerners saw him as an abolitionist hero. Most Southerners saw the raid as a violent attack on their right to own slaves.

John Brown (second from right) is captured by Marines at Harpers Ferry. His violent raid fuelled tension between the North and South prior to the Civil War.

Abraham Lincoln

When Abraham Lincoln, a Northerner who opposed slavery, became president of the United States in 1861, many of the Southern states had already withdrawn from the Union. In his inaugural speech he spoke about unity. Addressing the Southerners, he said: "In your hands, my dissatisfied fellow-countrymen, and not in mine, is the momentous issue of civil war." It was too late, however, to mend the rift between the North and South, and civil war broke out a month later.

Lincoln, who came from a poor family in Kentucky, believed above all else that the states should stay united.

Civil War Breaks Out

By the mid 1850s, slavery was a major issue for politicians (though not for most ordinary people) in the North and South. Some political leaders in the North wanted to see slavery banned throughout the country on moral grounds. Politicians in the South, many of whom owned slaves, felt their cotton-based economy and whole Southern culture were threatened by this. From 1860, eleven Southern states withdrew, or seceded, from the Union and formed the Confederate States of America (the Confederacy), led by President Jefferson Davis. The North, led by President Abraham Lincoln, denied them the right to secede, and went to war to preserve the Union.

The Civil War broke out on April 12, 1861, at the Union stronghold of Fort Sumter, shown here, in South Carolina. The Confederates fired on the fort after hearing it was to be sent more weapons, and the Union commander surrendered to them.

CIVIL WAR BREAKS OUT 29

Union general Ulysses S. Grant (seated) was unprepared when the Confederates attacked at Shiloh. His narrow victory enabled the Union army to push on down the Mississippi River to Vicksburg.

The Confederacy has the Upper Hand

The Confederacy won some major victories in Virginia, including the Battle of Bull Run (the name of a stream near Manassas) and Fredericksburg. In two battles at Bull Run in 1861 and 1862, Lee's hugely outnumbered Confederate troops pushed Union forces back to Washington, D.C. Later in 1862, Union forces attacked the town of Fredericksburg, where Lee's Confederate soldiers were waiting for them, entrenched in the hills. More than twice as many Union soldiers were killed as Confederates, and the Union was again forced to retreat.

The Battle of Shiloh

The Battle of Shiloh took place on the western front of the Civil War, in southwestern Tennessee, on 6–7 April, 1862. Confederate troops made a surprise attack on Union forces led by General Ulysses S. Grant (1822–85) and nearly defeated them. Although Union troops eventually won the battle, they were too exhausted to chase the Confederates as they retreated. With more than 23,000 casualties, it was the bloodiest battle of the Civil War to date.

Robert E. Lee

Confederate general Robert E. Lee won many battles by outsmarting his northern opponents. Although he was strongly loyal to his state of Virginia, he was actually a great believer in keeping the Union together. His strength, courage, and generosity made him a hero among his men and an enduring symbol of the South.

President Lincoln asked Lee to be the commander of the Union army in 1861, but Lee, loyal to his home state of Virginia, chose to fight for the Confederacy instead.

The Battle of Bull Run, on 21 July, 1861, was the first major land clash in the Civil War.

CIVIL WAR: EARLY BATTLES

1861
January
South Carolina, Mississippi, Florida, Alabama, Georgia, Louisiana, and Texas secede from the Union.

February
The Southern states create their own government and write a constitution.

April
Virginia, Arkansas, North Carolina, and Tennessee secede from the Union.

1862
March
The first battle between two ironclad ships ends in a stalemate.

May–August
General George McClellan leads Union troops in the Peninsular Campaign in Virginia. After initial victories his troops are defeated by Confederates.

September
In the Battle of Antietam, a Union victory, more than 16,000 men are killed in the bloodiest single day of the Civil War.

Civil War: The Conclusion

In 1863, President Lincoln's Emancipation Proclamation came into effect, freeing all slaves in the Confederate states. Some 180,000 black men joined the Union army as a result. Outraged, the Confederacy became more determined than ever to win the Civil War. Superb strategy, focus, and drive had enabled the Confederate army to win some major battles during the first three years of the war. But in the end, the sheer size of the Union army gave them the upper hand. At the Battle of Gettysburg, the tide of war turned in the Union's favor.

Slaves celebrate Lincoln's Emancipation Proclamation.

The Battle of Chancellorsville was a Confederate victory for General Lee, but it cost him nearly a quarter of his troops.

The Battle of Chancellorsville
In May 1863, a small Confederate army came up against a much larger Union army near Chancellorsville, in North Virginia. General Lee divided his Confederate force to try to out-maneuvre the Union army, which was commanded by "fighting Joe" Hooker (1814–79). Lee attacked the front of the Union army, while General Stonewall Jackson led a daring surprise attack on the right flank. The Union army was split in two and retreated three days later. The battle resulted in some 30,000 casualties.

Draft Riots in New York
In March 1863, the US Congress tightened the laws requiring most white men up to the age of 45 to join the army. Only those who could either hire a substitute or pay the government a fee of $300 were able to avoid the draft. Many New Yorkers were angered that the rich could buy their way out of going to war. Rioting broke out on 13 July, particularly among the Irish immigrants, who felt their jobs were threatened by the newly freed slaves. For five days angry mobs ran riot in the city.

New York rioters attacked newspaper offices and killed several black men. US troops had to be called in to stop the riots.

The Turning Point of the War
The Battle of Gettysburg was a major victory for the North and the turning point in the Civil War. Union forces under General George G. Meade (1815–72) defeated Lee's Confederate army in a three-day battle at the town of Gettysburg, Pennsylvania. Four months later, Lincoln delivered his famous Gettysburg Address. He finished his speech about equality, unity, and freedom by declaring: "government of the people, by the people, for the people, shall not perish from the Earth."

A Confederate soldier, in grey, attacks the Union standard-bearer at the Battle of Gettysburg in July 1863.

"Stonewall" Jackson
Robert E. Lee's best general, Thomas Jonathan "Stonewall" Jackson (1824–63), was known for his resourcefulness, self-control, and bravery. He won several battles in the Peninsular Campaign, as well as the Battles of Bull Run, Harpers Ferry, and Fredericksburg. In May 1863, during the Battle of Chancellorsville, another victory, he was accidentally shot by one of his own men and died a week later. Lee said of Jackson's death that it was like "losing my right arm."

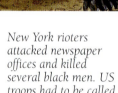

Jackson earned the nickname "Stonewall" during the first Battle of Bull Run, at which he held off a much larger Union army.

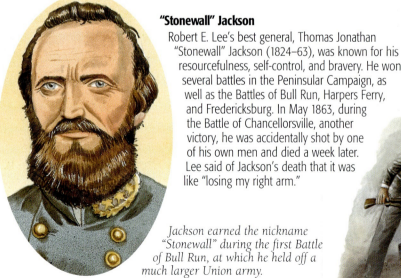

General Lee surrenders

Toward the end of the Civil War, Confederate forces, vastly outnumbered by Union men, began to falter. Their supply lines were cut, and they were hungry and exhausted. At the Appomattox Courthouse in North Virginia, Lee finally surrendered to General Ulysses S. Grant, marking the end of the Civil War. The war had lasted for four years and killed more than 630,000 men.

General Lee (seated left) surrenders at Appomattox Courthouse. By the terms of the agreement, Confederate soldiers were allowed to return to their homes in the South.

Lincoln's Assassination

The Civil War left the United States in a mess. President Lincoln knew he had a lot of mending to do, but he was denied the chance. On 14 April, 1865, just days after the Civil War ended, he was shot in the back of the head while watching a play at Ford's Theater in Washington, D.C. His assassin was a Southern patriot and actor named John Wilkes Booth.

The Washington war department offered a reward for Booth's capture. He was found hiding in a tobacco barn and was killed on 26 April, 1865.

Below: After crossing the Mississippi River in May 1863, Union general Ulysses S. Grant and his Army of the Tennessee drove the Confederates into defensive lines around the city of Vicksburg, which Grant then besieged for over a month. On Vicksburg's surrender, the Union gained control of the Mississippi River.

CIVIL WAR: THE CONCLUSION

1863

January
President Lincoln's Emancipation Proclamation bans slavery in the Confederate states. This was the first step toward abolishing slavery altogether.

March
The Union government passes a new draft law, sparking riots in New York and other cities.

July
General George E. Pickett leads a successful attack against the Confederate Army, clinching the Battle of Gettysburg for the Union.

November
The Union wins the Battle of Chattanooga in Tennessee.

1864
In September, Union troops, led by General William Tecumseh Sherman (1820–1891), capture Atlanta, Georgia.

1865
On April 9, Lee surrenders at Appomattox, officially ending the Civil War. In May, the last Confederate troops surrender.

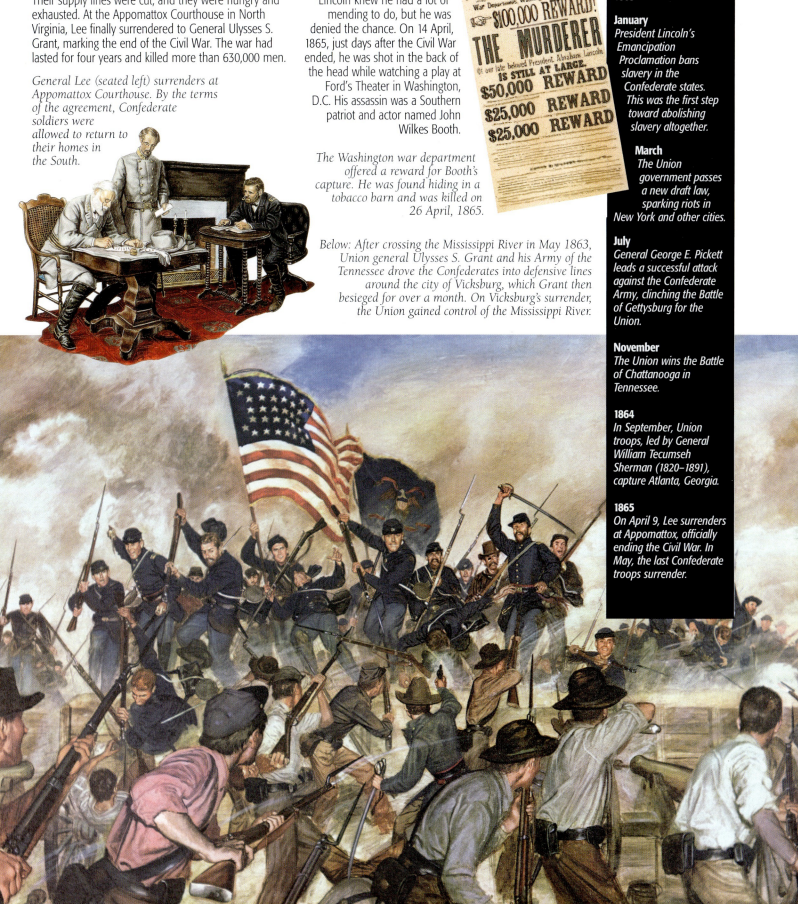

Reconstruction Era

After the Civil War, the South was in ruins. The government of President Andrew Johnson faced some major challenges, including rebuilding the South and bringing the Southern states back into the Union. This period, which lasted from 1865 to 1877, is known as the Reconstruction era. Although all the Southern states rejoined the Union and began to repair the damage, life changed little for many of the four million freed slaves, who faced poverty and discrimination.

RECONSTRUCTION ERA

1865
Andrew Johnson becomes the 17th US president.

1866
In April, Congress passes the Civil Rights Act in response to the Southern Black Codes. In May, the Ku Klux Klan (an organization promoting "white supremacy") is formed by Southern Civil War veterans. Its members terrorize and kill black Americans.

1868
The fourteenth amendment grants citizenship and other basic rights to former slaves.

1869
Ulysses S. Grant becomes the 18th US president.

1870
The fifteenth amendment guarantees voting rights to former slaves.

c. 1876
The Jim Crow laws are introduced, reversing reconstruction civil rights acts. These laws are supposed to make black communities "separate but equal," but in reality make black Americans second-class citizens.

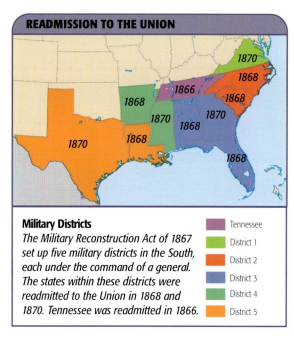

READMISSION TO THE UNION

Military Districts
The Military Reconstruction Act of 1867 set up five military districts in the South, each under the command of a general. The states within these districts were readmitted to the Union in 1868 and 1870. Tennessee was readmitted in 1866.

- Tennessee
- District 1
- District 2
- District 3
- District 4
- District 5

Carpetbaggers and Scalawags

After the Civil War, many Northerners moved to the South seeking opportunities to make money. They became known as "carpetbaggers," because they traveled with all their possessions in inexpensive bags made of carpet. Many joined the Republican Party, along with Southern white Republicans (known as "scalawags") and freed slaves, or Freedmen. The three groups formed a coalition in the state and local governments to push for civil rights and voting rights for the freed slaves.

Some corrupt carpetbaggers gained a bad name for taking advantage of freed slaves.

The North Prospers

In contrast to the South, the North thrived during the 1860s and 1870s. The Civil War had actually stimulated manufacturing and business, and technological advances in machinery made farming easier. Many Northerners were growing rich and finding time for leisure pursuits. In New York, Leonard Jerome, "The King of Wall Street," helped found the American Jockey Club and built the Jerome Park Racetrack in the Bronx.

Jerome Park Racetrack in the late 1860s. Jerome was the maternal grandfather of the British Prime Minister, Winston Churchill (1874–1965).

A portrait of President Andrew Johnson (1808–75), who oversaw the reconstruction of the United States after the Civil War.

Three Phases

During the first phase of Reconstruction, known as Presidential Reconstruction (1865–66), President Johnson persuaded the Southern states to rejoin the Union, despite opposition from radical Republicans. During the second phase, known as Radical Reconstruction (1866–73), Congress passed the 14th amendment to the Constitution, which gave freed slaves civil rights, and the 15th amendment, which allowed them to vote in political elections. In the third phase, called "Redemption" (1873–77), white "supremacist" Southerners defeated the Republicans and took control of the South.

RECONSTRUCTION ERA 33

Black Codes

For many of the four million slaves who suddenly gained their freedom by the Emancipation Act, life in fact became harder than it had been before. Most freed slaves had no money or formal education, and they were treated worse than ever by hostile white people. Then, in 1865 and 1866, the Southern states passed laws called "Black Codes," which severely limited their rights. The government responded by passing Reconstruction Acts in 1867 that put the Southern states back under military control and forced them to grant rights to blacks.

A night train on the Hudson River Railroad in New York state.

CROSSING THE CONTINENT

PROMONTORY, UTAH
OMAHA, NEBRASKA
SACRAMENTO, CALIFORNIA

— Central Pacific
— Union Pacific
— Added later

The Railroads

The world's first transcontinental railroad was completed in 1869. Two companies built the western portion. The Union Pacific company lay tracks going westward from Nebraska, while the Central Pacific Company lay tracks heading east from California. The tracks met at Promontory, Utah. The final spike to be hammered into the line was made of gold.

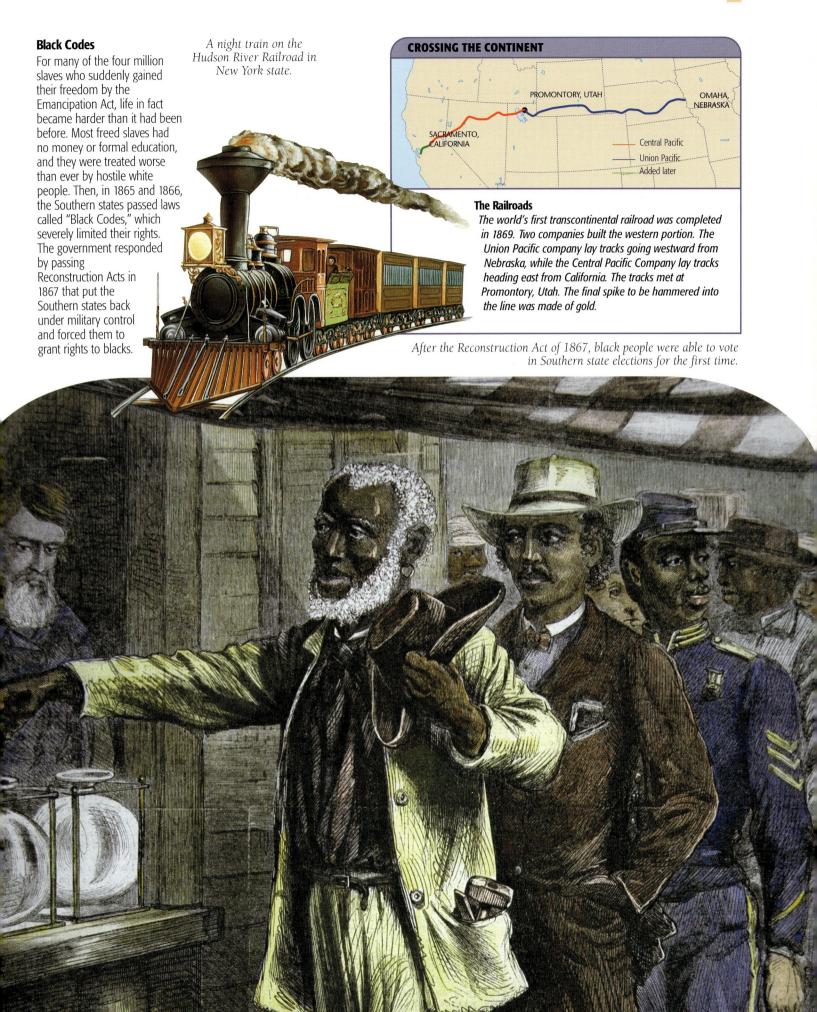

After the Reconstruction Act of 1867, black people were able to vote in Southern state elections for the first time.

Native Americans Forced Out

After the Civil War was over, American settlers once again began to head west, lured by the prospects of land, money, and adventure on the frontier. The land they wanted to settle, however, was the homeland of many western Native American tribes. For 25 years the United States battled against the Sioux, the Nez Percé, and the Apaches, finally succeeding in confining them to reservations. By taking their lands and killing the buffalo on which they depended, the white settlers won the West.

Chief Joseph (1840–1904) said in his famous surrender speech: "Hear me, my chiefs! My heart is sick and sad. From where the Sun now stands, I will fight no more forever."

A photograph of trader Jesse Chisholm, who drove a wagon across Oklahoma to set up a trading post in Kansas. His route became known as the Chisholm Trail.

The Nez Percé

Gold seekers invaded the first Nez Percé (French for "pierced nose") reservation in the 1860s. The government tried to move the Nez Percé people to a smaller reservation, but they resisted, and in 1877 a group led by Chief Joseph clashed with US army forces. Joseph and his people headed for Canada, marching some 1,400 miles (2,250 km), but were forced to surrender near the border.

The Chisholm Trail

In the late 1860s, settlers in the West were keeping vast numbers of cattle on the prairie grasslands. To get them to markets in the east, cowboys would drive the cattle for about 1,000 miles (1,600 km) across the open prairies from near San Antonio, Texas, north to Abilene in Kansas. At Abilene, trains stopped to pick up the cattle and take them east. Between 1867 and 1871, about 1.5 million head of cattle were driven along the Chisholm Trail, as it was known. Abilene grew into a boisterous town typical of the Wild West.

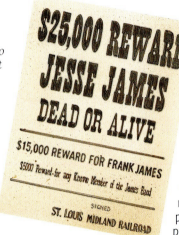

A "wanted" poster for Jesse James (1847–82).

Jesse James

Outlaws were one of the many dangers faced by the pioneers. Jesse James is probably the most famous of them. He and his gang held up trains, stagecoaches, banks, and shops at gunpoint and took people's money. When a reward was offered for the capture of Jesse or his brother Frank, dead or alive, one of their own gang shot Jesse in the head.

Apaches Moved to Reservations

For 25 years the United States army fought against Native American tribes to try to force them onto reservations. The Apaches of New Mexico and Texas, who were nomadic and not used to having to stay in one place, fought long and hard to keep their way of life. Apache resistance ended when the ferocious Chief Geronimo (1829–1909) surrendered in 1886. He later appeared at the 1904 World's Fair, selling souvenirs of himself.

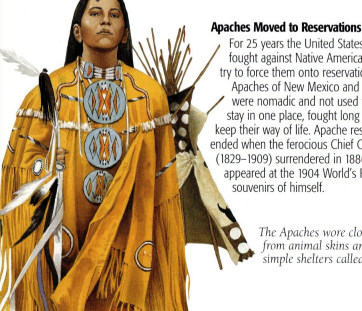

The Apaches wore clothing made from animal skins and lived in simple shelters called tepees.

Sioux warriors wore deerskin shirts, often decorated with beads and feathers.

Custer's Last Stand
At the Battle of Little Bighorn (below), also known as "Custer's Last Stand," Civil War hero George Armstrong Custer (1839–76) led an attack against Sioux and Cheyenne warriors, including chiefs Crazy Horse and Sitting Bull. The Native Americans swiftly killed Custer and his whole unit. The death of their hero angered many whites and fuelled the campaign to force the Native Americans onto reservations.

NATIVE AMERICANS FORCED OUT

1862
The Homestead Act grants free land to settlers in the West. After five years, a settler can claim 160 acres (65 hectares) if he or she has built a house on it, dug a well, plowed 10 acres (4 hectares) and lived there.

1865
The Navajo surrender and are settled on a New Mexico reservation.

1877
The Nez Percé are forced to move to a smaller reservation. In response, Nez Percé warriors kill four white men, sparking the Nez Percé war.

1877
Sioux chief Crazy Horse surrenders to United States troops.

1881
The Missouri governor offers a reward for the capture of the notorious outlaw Jesse James.

1886
The Apache Wars end with the surrender of Chief Geronimo.

A Native American artist paints a scene of a ritual dance on to buffalo hide.

Left: A poster for Buffalo Bill's show, which romanticized the culture of the "Wild West."

"Buffalo Bill" Cody
William Frederick Cody (1846–1917) was the most famous buffalo hunter in the West. His amazing skill earned him the nickname "Buffalo Bill." From 1867 to 1868 he killed more than 4,000 buffalo for food for the workers on the Union Pacific Railroad. He worked as an army scout, hunting guide and actor in a traveling show called "Buffalo Bill's Wild West."

Hunting the Buffalo
Vast herds of buffalo roamed the prairies before whites settled there. The tens of millions of buffalo provided the Native Americans with meat for food and hides for clothing. In the late 1800s, however, white hunters killed them in their millions, and by 1889 the buffalo population was nearly extinct. One main aim of the hunters was to deprive the Native Americans of their main source of food so that they would have to agree to live on reservations.

Immigration

America in the mid 1800s was regarded by people all over the world as a land of opportunity and freedom. Millions decided to leave their own countries and move there to escape persecution, or the hunger and poverty caused by crop failures and unemployment. Between 1870 and 1900, nearly 12 million immigrants arrived. German, Irish, British, and Scandinavian immigrants initially dominated, supplanted after 1900 by Italians, Austro-Hungarians, and Russians. Public services such as state schools soon developed to cope with the rise in population.

The Beach Pneumatic Transit used a giant fan to propel its single underground rail carriage.

Some 40,000 Italians arrived in the USA between 1850 and 1880, largely from northern Italy. Many southern Italians came later.

New Transport for Cities

Immigrants poured into the cities looking for work, and soon new transportation systems were developed to ease congestion in the streets. In New York City, Alfred Ely Beach demonstrated his underground pneumatic train, the city's first underground railway, in 1870, and in the same year overland steam trains first ran a regular service.

The Immigrant Experience

Asian immigrants generally arrived on the West Coast and European immigrants on the East. Many had made long, difficult journeys by steamship and arrived with few possessions and little money. On arrival, they often encountered hostility from Americans who were suspicious of them because they looked different and worked hard for little money. Groups of immigrants often ended up in the worst neighborhoods, for example the Five Points slum in New York.

The Chinese Exclusion Act

The Chinese Exclusion Act, passed in 1882, marked the end of the US policy of welcoming immigrants from all over the world. Chinese immigrants escaping poverty and political persecution in China had been particularly drawn to California, where they made money working in the gold fields or building the transcontinental railroads. Many Californians resented them for taking their jobs and driving down wages. The Chinese Exclusion Act prohibited the immigration of Chinese laborers. It was renewed in 1892 and again in 1902.

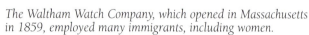

The Waltham Watch Company, which opened in Massachusetts in 1859, employed many immigrants, including women.

A Chinese immigrant working in a Californian gold field in 1849.

Work in Factories and Mines

Manufacturing was thriving in the northeastern USA at this time. Factories often employed immigrants because they were prepared to do dangerous jobs for low pay. On the East Coast, people from Ireland, Italy, Poland, and Russia often worked in grim conditions, but earned more than they were able to in their own countries. Women made up a large part of the workforce. In the West, Chinese immigrants worked as miners, which was often perilous.

IMMIGRATION

1819
Immigration statistics are officially recorded for the first time.

1845
In Ireland, the potato famine causes nearly 500,000 Irish to emigrate to the United States.

1848
Many political refugees from the revolution in Germany immigrate to the United States.

1849
Chinese immigrants pour into the United States as part of the California Gold Rush.

1862
Scandinavian immigrants pour into the Midwest in response to the Homestead Act.

1880
Crop failures and poverty in Italy lead to a wave of Italian immigrants, who number nearly 4 million.

1882
The Immigration Act restricts Chinese immigration and bans ex-convicts, mentally disabled people, and those unable to look after themselves.

1885
Congress bans the immigration of contract laborers.

1891
The Bureau of Immigration is established.

Oklahoma Land Rush

After the Homestead Act of 1862 (see page 35), which offered free land to settlers, many landless immigrants headed west to claim a piece of land. In 1889 some particularly good land, serviced by a railroad and water towers, was offered in Oklahoma. At 12 noon on 22 April, people were admitted across the borders with Arkansas and Texas to claim a part of this land. The resulting town of Guthrie grew from a population of zero to more than 10,000 in a single afternoon.

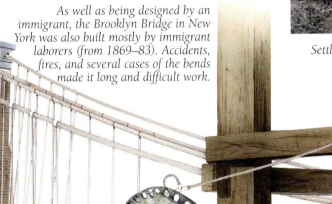

As well as being designed by an immigrant, the Brooklyn Bridge in New York was also built mostly by immigrant laborers (from 1869–83). Accidents, fires, and several cases of the bends made it long and difficult work.

Settlers lay claim to a plot of land at Guthrie, which became the first capital of Oklahoma.

Specialized Kinds of Work

Different ethnic groups tended to specialize in particular areas of work. The Slavs, for example, became steel workers, the Greeks opened small shops, the Jews in New York often worked in tailoring or ran delicatessens. In Boston, New York, and Chicago, many city jobs were done by German immigrants, like John Roebling (1806–69), who designed the Brooklyn Bridge.

Ellis Island

On the East Coast, the first immigration center was opened at Castle Garden, New York, in 1855, and it operated until 1890. It was replaced by Ellis Island, where nearly 12 million immigrants were processed between 1892 and 1954. Immigrants were interviewed and had to pass medical exams before being admitted to the United States, but only two percent were turned away. Today, more than 40 percent of Americans have ancestors who came through Ellis Island.

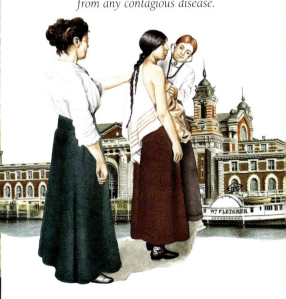

Immigrants at Ellis Island were checked to make sure they weren't suffering from any contagious disease.

End of the Century: Money and Ideas

Toward the end of the century, new inventions and modern business practices were changing the way people lived in the United States. More people than ever lived in cities, due to continued immigration and migration from the countryside. Suburbs developed to provide more comfortable surroundings for those who could afford them. A few people became extremely rich, but the poor suffered in terrible working and living conditions.

Edison's phonograph recorded messages and played them back.

George Washington Carver
The lifelong vocation of the agricultural chemist George Washington Carver was simple: he wanted to help black farmers. At the Tuskegee Institute he developed a remarkable number of ways to use the traditional crops of the South, including more than 300 uses for peanuts, such as for ink, plastic, and soap, and more than 100 uses for sweet potatoes, such as for rubber and glue.

A portrait of George Washington Carver (1864–1943), who helped the South become less dependent on cotton.

Rich and Poor
Toward the end of the century, the gap between rich and poor grew tremendously. By developing innovations in steel production, one man, a Scottish immigrant named Andrew Carnegie, became the richest man in the world. He earned about 4,000 times more than his steel workers, who worked long shifts in boiling hot temperatures for about $10 a week. Poor working conditions led to reform movements in the early 20th century.

Gold Fever
In 1897, gold was discovered near the town of Dawson in the Yukon region of Canada. Many Americans traveled there to strike it rich. The population of the town grew to more than 30,000, but only about 4,000 people actually discovered gold.

A gold seeker pans for gold in the Canadian wilderness.

The Spanish-American War
At the end of the century, there was a major shift in ideas in America toward imperialism. For the first time, the country was beginning to look at itself as a force in the world. In 1898, this mood, combined with the nation's need to protect its sugar trade with the Spanish colony of Cuba—which was seeking independence—led America to declare war on Spain. In the first major battle, Commodore George Dewey led a naval victory against Spanish forces in the Philippines without the loss of a single American life. US forces then easily defeated the Spanish in sea and land battles in Cuba and Puerto Rico. By the Treaty of Paris, Cuba became an independent country, and the United States gained the former Spanish colonies of Guam, Puerto Rico, and the Philippines.

END OF THE CENTURY: MONEY AND IDEAS

The Centennial Exhibition
To celebrate the 100th birthday of the USA in 1876, a huge exhibition was held in Philadelphia, Pennsylvania. The highlight was the Machinery Hall, which featured all kinds of new technology, including a telephone, a typewriter, an electric light, and the giant Corliss steam engine.

Socialite Alice Vanderbilt, inspired by the new electric lighting, attended her family's fancy dress ball in 1883 as "Electric Light."

The art gallery at the Centennial Exhibition, the first World's Fair held in the United States.

Andrew Carnegie (1835-1919), the "father of American dream."

Below: A naval parade held in honor of George Dewey (1837–1917), who became a national hero for his role in the Spanish-American War.

END OF THE CENTURY: MONEY AND IDEAS

1876
Alexander Graham Bell (1847–1922), a Scottish emigrant to the United States, patents the telephone.

1884
In Chicago, building begins on the Home Insurance Building, one of the world's first skyscrapers.

1886
The American Federation of Labor (now The American Federation of Labor and Congress of Industrial Organizations (AFL-CIO) is founded. Atlanta pharmacist John Styth Pemberton (1831–88) invents the drink Coca Cola.

1888
George Eastman (1854–1932) introduces the Kodak camera. Thomas Edison invents the kinetoscope, the first machine to produce motion pictures by a rapid succession of individual views.

1896
Henry Ford introduces his first automobile.

Art, Music, and Literature

During the early 19th century, the arts in America tended to favor classical and European styles. The art movement known as the Hudson River School and the literary movement known as Transcendentalism celebrated America's natural beauty. By the late 1860s, slavery and the Civil War were having an influence, and increasingly artists and writers were expressing the hardships people faced. Slave narratives by Frederick Douglass and Harriet Jacobs exposed the cruelties of slavery, while in music, ragtime and the blues reflected the experience of many black Americans.

Above: Thomas Cole of the Hudson River School used light to dramatic effect in his oil painting "Landscape (Moonlight)" c. 1833–34.

ART, MUSIC, AND LITERATURE

1826
America's first major novelist, James Fenimore Cooper (1789–1851), publishes his classic pioneer novel *The Last of the Mohicans*.

1828
Noah Webster publishes the *American Dictionary of the English Language*, which promotes American (as opposed to British English) spellings and usage.

1845
Abolitionist Frederick Douglass (1818–95) publishes his memoirs of life spent as a slave.

1872
The Metropolitan Museum of Art first opens in New York City.

1895
Stephen Crane (1871–1900) publishes his Civil War novel *The Red Badge of Courage*.

1899
Scott Joplin's "Maple Leaf Rag" becomes a hit.

The Hudson River School
A number of artists in the early 19th century who painted the beauty and grandeur of nature in a realistic and detailed way became known as the Hudson River School. Their style is considered to be the first truly American style of painting. The founder of the movement was Thomas Cole (1801–48), who painted scenes of the Catskill Mountains above the Hudson River in New York state. Other Hudson River artists included Thomas Doughty and Asher Durand.

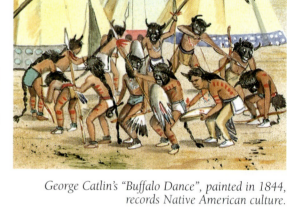

George Catlin's "Buffalo Dance", painted in 1844, records Native American culture.

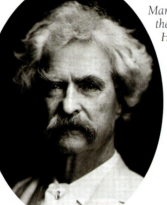

Mark Twain grew up in the small town of Hannibal, Missouri.

Realism
One of the first American realists was the great American writer Mark Twain (1835–1910, born Samuel Langhorne Clemens), who portrayed life on the Mississippi River in novels such as *The Adventures of Tom Sawyer*. Realists wrote about the good and bad in people and everyday events in an objective way; they were neither romantic nor sentimental, and generally made no moral judgements.

Daniel Chester French (1850–1931) designed this 65-foot (20-m) tall statue, "The Republic," for the Columbian Exhibition of 1893, held in Chicago, Illinois.

George Catlin
George Catlin (1796–1872) painted scenes of Native American life that have become an important historical record of their heritage. After traveling with famous explorer William Clark into Native American territory in 1830, Catlin spent the next few years on the Great Plains, painting more than 500 scenes of Native American life.

Two Popular Styles
Neo-classical art and architecture, modelled on examples from ancient Greece and Rome, were popular in 19th-century America. Examples include many plantation houses in the South, and also the Lincoln Memorial in Washington, D.C. Naturalistic sculptures, such as those by Augustus Saint-Gaudens (1848–1907), celebrated patriotic subjects and Civil War heroes.

ART, MUSIC, AND LITERATURE 41

The Transcendentalists
A famous group of philosophers, writers, and social reformers lived in the town of Concord, near Boston, Massachusetts. Known as the Transcendentalists, they included Ralph Waldo Emerson (1803–82) and Henry David Thoreau (1817–62). Emerson wrote about self-reliance and finding truth in nature. Thoreau, who spent more than two years living in a one-room cabin in the woods near Concord, wrote about the value of living simply and protesting against injustice by breaking the rules. His writings on civil disobedience inspired future leaders, including Martin Luther King, Jr. (1929–68).

Portrait of Ralph Waldo Emerson.

Ragtime and Blues
Two important kinds of music were developed by black Southerners in the late 19th century, and they continue to influence popular music today. Ragtime featured melodies with uneven beats, usually on the piano. Scott Joplin (1868–1917), the "King of Ragtime," became famous for his "Maple Leaf Rag" in 1899. Blues (singing or playing to a particular rhythm) may have developed from "field hollers"–the calls that black plantation workers made to each other. Blues had a major influence on the development of jazz.

A poster for Scott Joplin's rag "The Entertainer," published in 1902. It remains a popular piano tune today.

Louisa May Alcott
Jo March, the heroine of Louisa May Alcott's *Little Women* (1869), is one of the great characters of American children's fiction. Alcott's autobiographical novel tells the story of four sisters living in New England during the Civil War. Alcott grew up in Concord among the Transcendentalists, who included her father, Bronson Alcott. She became a social reformer and worked to gain the vote for women.

A scene from the 1994 film Little Women, based on the hugely popular novel by Louisa May Alcott (1832–88). Jo March was the first really individual young heroine in American fiction.

Canada: Peoples and Rebellions

CANADA: PEOPLES AND REBELLIONS

1812
The British in Canada support the Native Americans and First Nations peoples whose land is being taken by American settlers. America invades Canada and fights the British in the War of 1812 (see pages 12–13).

1816
A Hudson's Bay Company governor is killed by Métis allies of the North West Company. This marks the birth of the Métis nation.

1821
Montreal businessman James McGill (1744–1813) endows McGill University.

1829
The first Welland Canal is completed, linking Lake Erie to Lake Ontario.

1831
Quebec City and Montreal are officially incorporated as cities.

1834
Toronto is officially incorporated as a city.

1836
The Champlain and St Lawrence Railroad, Canada's first railway, is officially opened.

Native Peoples
Canada was already inhabited by many different native peoples before the Europeans arrived. There were native Indians, or First Nations, living throughout the region and speaking a number of different languages. And in the cold, far northwest were the Inuit, who survived by hunting and fishing. Many Europeans married native peoples, and their descendants were known as Métis. The Métis developed their own language, and mixed native and European traditions.

The thunderbird is a powerful mythical creature in many First Nations cultures.

1818 TREATY WITH BRITAIN

- British
- American
- Spanish
- Russian

The 49th Parallel
In 1818, the Anglo-American Convention established the border between the British Canadian colonies and the United States. The boundary was latitude 49 degrees north, called the 49th parallel. It stretched from the Lake of the Woods (where Ontario, Manitoba, and Minnesota meet) west to the Rocky Mountains.

Red River Settlement
In the early 1800s, Scottish philanthropist Thomas Douglas, 5th Earl of Selkirk, obtained a grant of land from the Hudson's Bay Company in Canada to found a new settlement for some of the poor farmers of Scotland and Northern Ireland. The first settlers arrived in 1812, and more came in 1815. Rival fur traders from the North West Company and many native peoples were hostile to the settlers, and killed 22 of them at the massacre of Seven Oaks (1816). The settlement recovered, however, and prospered.

Miles Macdonnell (1769–1828) officially established the Red River colony of Assiniboia and became its first governor.

Canada: Peoples and Rebellions

After the American War of Independence, thousands of colonists who were loyal to the British fled north to Canada. The region already had a large French population—French settlers had arrived in the 17th century—as well as its own native First Nations and Inuit peoples. Conflicts inevitably arose, particularly over land ownership, and battles were fought between the First Nations, supported by the British, and the Americans. The borders changed many times, and increasingly Canada's peoples began to share a common goal: the desire for self-rule.

Hudson's Bay Company fur trappers traveled on foot through forests and across mountains, as well as by canoe along Canada's extensive rivers. Among the animals they caught were beavers. The beaver fur was made into felt and used to make hats for the European market.

Trading Companies Unite

Two fur trading firms, the Hudson's Bay Company and the North West Company, were keen rivals during the late 1700s and early 1800s. They used any means, including vandalism, bribery, and violence, to compete to sell more furs. Most of their resources were going into fighting each other, so in 1821 the British government took measures to merge them into one company under the Hudson's Bay name. Today, Hudson's Bay is still one of Canada's most powerful companies.

Rebellions of 1837

In the early 1800s, Upper Canada (now Ontario) and Lower Canada (now Quebec) were both governed by cliques of rich people. Many people became angry by the self-serving policies of these powerful people, and in 1837 groups in both provinces revolted. William Lyon Mackenzie (1795–1861) led the revolt in Upper Canada and Louis Joseph Papineau (1786–1871) in Lower Canada. Although the revolts were quashed by the governments, they led to many reforms, including the Act of Union, which united Upper and Lower Canada in 1840.

Rebels seized weapons from a Toronto armory and marched down Yonge Street, sparking Upper Canada's rebellion of 1837.

CANADA: UNION AND CONSTITUTION

1846
The Oregon Boundary Treaty establishes a border between British North America and the United States at 49 degrees north latitude.

1853
The Grand Trunk Railroad between Montreal and Portland, Maine, is completed, creating North America's first international railroad.

1854
The Reciprocity Treaty abolishes customs tariffs and helps increase trade between Canada and the United States.

1879
Sir John A. Macdonald (1815–91), the first prime minister of Canada, encourages westward expansion and growth in manufacturing.

1897–98
Miners seeking gold pour into the Klondike (Yukon Territory), (see page 38).

A Shortage of Labor

During the 1840s, Canada had a shortage of labor. Thousands of French-Canadians were emigrating from Canada to the USA, and there simply weren't enough people to farm the vast open prairies efficiently. The invention of a new horse-drawn reaping machine by American inventor Cyrus H. McCormick dramatically changed farming in the region from the 1850s onward. This once labor-intensive task was now able to be done much more quickly.

Cyrus H. McCormick (1809–84) and his reaping machine in 1837. The machine was distributed widely on the new railways that were being built, and was demonstrated to farmers by a vast network of trained salesmen.

The Act of Union

Following the rebellions of 1837 (see pages 43), the British government sent John Lambton, 1st Earl of Durham (1792–1840) to investigate the colonial governments. In his famous report, Lord Durham gave details of economic problems and conflicts between the English and the French people. He recommended a union between Upper Canada and Lower Canada. The Act of Union, passed in 1840 and enacted in 1841, joined Upper and Lower Canada as the Province of Canada.

Confederation and a New Railway

In 1867, the 1840 Act of Union was replaced by the British North America Act, which united the Province of Canada (Ontario and Quebec) with the colonies of New Brunswick and Nova Scotia. In 1871, the province of British Columbia on the west coast agreed to join this Confederation. The government, in return, took on the colony's debt and agreed to extend the Canadian Pacific Railway to British Columbia. Workers on the railway had to contend with treacherous mountain conditions and a shortage of money, but in 1885 Canada's first transcontinental railroad was completed. The main line ran between Montreal in the east and Port Moody, just outside Vancouver, in the west.

Thousands of Chinese laborers worked long hours for little pay building the Canadian Pacific Railroad.

Canada: Union and Constitution

For the British government, the Canadian colonies were a problem: unrest was widespread, and economic progress was slow, especially compared to the United States. The government decided that the best course would be to unite the provinces and create a system of self-government. Expansion and economic advances soon followed, and by the British North America Act of 1867 the region officially became known as Canada. The same act set out Canada's Constitution, defining such things as its federal structure and its justice and taxation systems.

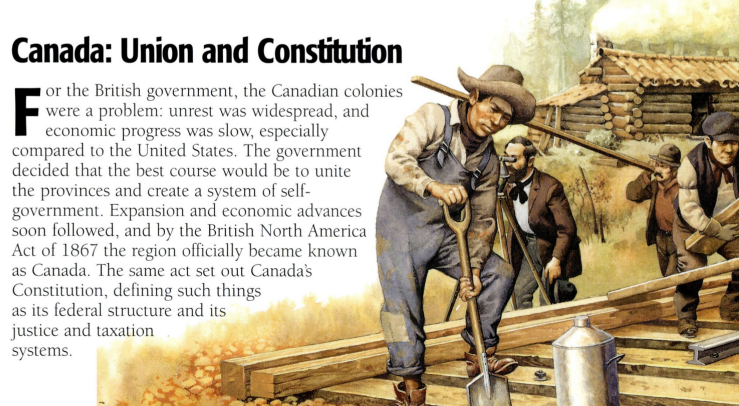

The "Mounties"

In 1873, Canada's first prime minister, Sir John A. Macdonald, created the North West Mounted Police (known as the "Mounties"). The force was organized like a British cavalry regiment, and its aim was to bring law and order to the Northwest Territories, where American whisky traders were causing trouble. The Mounties also kept order during the building of the Canadian Pacific Railway and the Klondike Gold Rush, and they enforced the law on the First Nations peoples, with whom they developed good relations.

The North West Mounted Police wore striking red jackets and stetson-style hats.

THE DOMINION OF CANADA

- Canada, 1867
- Territory added 1870
- Provinces added by 1873
- Territory added 1880
- British crown colony
- Canadian territorial claim surrendered to USA

Provinces and Territories

In 1867, the Confederation of Canada's four provinces (Ontario, Quebec, New Brunswick, and Nova Scotia) created "one Dominion under the name of Canada." This area was hugely enlarged in 1870, when the Hudson's Bay Company transferred to the government of Canada an area around Hudson's Bay known as Rupert's Land and the vast North-Western Territory (the two regions now formed the Northwest Territories). The province of Manitoba was also created and joined the Confederation in 1870. It was followed by British Columbia in 1871 and Prince Edward Island in 1873. Yukon Territory joined in 1898.

Glossary

Abolitionists People who believed strongly that slavery and the laws that permitted it should be abolished (got rid of).

Barbary pirates Sea robbers from North Africa led by the Bey (ruler) of Tripoli. For 150 years they menaced ships in the Mediterranean.

Black Codes Laws passed in the Southern states in 1865–66 that gave freed slaves a few civil rights, but denied them many others, including education.

Bounty hunters Men who made a living from hunting down runaway slaves and claiming the reward money offered by their owners. In the West, bounty hunters pursued outlaws for government rewards.

Civil rights The rights to which a country's citizens are entitled: they include education and the vote. Acts to extend Black rights in the US were passed in 1866, 1875, 1957 and 1964.

Confederate States The 11 Southern states that seceded from the Union in 1860–61: Alabama, Florida, Georgia, Louisiana, Mississippi, South and North Carolina, Texas, Arkansas, Tennessee and Virginia.

Congress The body of the US government responsible for making laws, producing a budget and passing bills. It also has the power to declare war. It is divided into the House of Representatives and the Senate.

Constitution The written guide to the government of the US. It came into force in 1789. Amendments (changes) since then include the abolition of slavery and granting the vote to Black people and women.

Contract laborers People without a settled job who would sign a contract with an employer to work for a short time, and then move on.

Corliss steam engine A huge 1400 horsepower engine made by US inventor George Henry Corliss, which for six months continuously drove all the machines used in the Centennial Exhibition of 1876.

Declaration of Sentiments Issued in 1848, this was the first public demand by women for equal rights with men, including the right to vote.

Expansionist policy The efforts made by Thomas Jefferson to move people out from the original 13 states on the East Coast into the largely unexplored north, south and west of the US – home to many Native American peoples. Congress passed laws to make sure land was fairly divided among white settlers.

Feminists Women who campaigned from the 1840s onwards for all women to have equal rights with men, including the rights to vote and to have their own money and property.

Founding Fathers The 55 men from the 13 original states who in 1787 drew up the Constitution of the US.

Frontier The borders of the US states settled by Whites. On the other side were Native American lands and wilderness. All through the 1800s, the government encouraged people to push back the frontier by settling and farming these lands.

Fugitive Slave Law Laws providing for the return of runaway slaves to their masters. First passed in 1793, these laws were often ignored by northern states once slavery had been abolished there. In 1850, harsher laws were aimed at closing the Underground Railroad. All these laws were repealed (cancelled) by Lincoln in 1864.

Gettysburg Address A short but immortal speech made by Lincoln in 1863, when he dedicated a cemetery and memorial to the soldiers killed in the recent battle.

Gin/ginning cotton The gin (its name comes from "engine") was a machine that made it possible for the first time to process a type of short-fibered cotton grown easily in the South.

Great Migration of 1843 The move westwards by pioneer families on the Oregon Trail to settle the regions bordering the Pacific.

Hitching post A wooden post or rail to which a horse can be tied.

Jim Crow laws Named after a "minstrel show" of 1828, these state laws were passed between 1881 and the 1950s to prevent Blacks and Whites from mixing in places such as theatres, schools, hotels and on public transport.

Kansas-Nebraska Act An Act of Congress passed in 1854 to allow settlers in the two new territories to vote whether to enter the Union as "free" or slave-owning states. Both were eventually admitted as free states.

Ku Klux Klan A secret society founded in the South in 1866 to prevent Blacks from owning land or using their right to vote. Members wore white sheets and pointed hoods to disguise themselves and were responsible for killing many Blacks without facing trial (lynchings).

Lawn jockey A hitching post carved and painted to look like a Black jockey. It would have stood on the lawn of a house. Escaping slaves could recognize a safe house by such a feature.

Merchant ships Ships with few or no guns, built and used for carrying goods to other countries for trade. They were always vulnerable to attack by pirates or enemy shipping.

Missouri Compromise A series of Acts of Congress (1820–21) that admitted Missouri to the Union as a slave state, but prohibited slavery elsewhere in the northern part of the Louisiana Purchase lands. This drew a precise line between slave and non-slave ("free") areas.

Outlaws People whose bad deeds put them outside the protection of the law. In the West, after the Civil War, outlaws such as the James brothers and Billy the Kid lived by robbery and murder, and died miserably, but later became the heroes of stories and films.

Pioneers People who "go where no-one has gone before", particularly the brave explorers and settler families who in the 1800s left the safety of the eastern US for unknown lands in the West. Early settlers in Canada, too, were pioneers.

Placer mining A method of excavating that uses water to remove heavy minerals such as gold from the sand and gravel deposits along the slower parts of fast-moving streams and rivers.

Republican Party One of the two main political parties of the US (the other is the Democratic Party). It was founded in 1854 as a result of political unrest after the Kansas-Nebraska Act. It won its first presidential election with Abraham Lincoln in 1860.

Reservation An area of land set aside by the US government for Native Americans, who were forced by law to settle there.

Spanish Empire By 1800 the Spanish, whose South American colonies dated from the 1500s, had moved into North America. They controlled Florida and most of the southwest. By 1850 nearly all their lands belonged to the US.

Supremacist A person who believed that White Americans should be "supreme" (in top place) and Black citizens should be denied their rights under the law.

Transcendentalism A way of thinking important in New England in the 1840s. It holds that humans should rely less on material possessions and more on the life of ideas.

Tribute Money paid to a ruler by another country in order to protect that country's citizens from attack.

Union The official body of colonies that joined together to form the United States.

Index

abolitionists 7, 24, 26, 27, 28, 40
Adams, John (President) 8
Africa 8, 9, 24
African Americans (*see also* slaves/slavery) 5
Alamo, the 16, 17
Alcott, Bronson 41
Alcott, Louisa May 41
Algeria 9
American War of Independence 14, 42
Anglo-American Convention 42
antebellum 22
Anthony, Susan B. 26
Antigua 7
Appomattox 31
Argentina 16
Assiniboia 42

Barbary pirates 8, 9
Barbary Wars 8, 9
Battles
 – Alamo, the (siege) 16, 17
 – Antietam 29
 – Beaverdams 13
 – Bull Run 29, 30
 – Burnt Corn 14
 – Chancellorsville 30
 – Chattanooga 31
 – Fort Mims (massacre) 14
 – Fredericksburg 29, 30
 – Gettysburg 30, 31
 – Harpers Ferry 28, 30
 – Horseshoe Bend 14
 – Lake Erie 13
 – Little Bighorn (Custer's Last Stand) 35
 – New Orleans 13
 – Queenston Heights 12, 13
 – San Jacinto 16
 – Seven Oaks (massacre) 42
 – Shiloh 29
 – Thames 13
 – Tippecanoe 12
 – Vicksburg (siege) 29, 31
Beach, Alfred Ely 36
Bell, Alexander Graham 39
Black Codes 32, 33
blues 41
Booth, John Wilkes 31
Bowie, Jim 17
Britain/British 5, 6, 8, 9, 12, 23, 42, 43, 44, 45

Brock, Isaac, Sir (Major General) 12, 13
Brown, John 28
buffalo 34, 35
Buffalo Bill 35

Calhoun, John C. (Vice President) 23
Canada 10, 12, 13, 18, 24, 25, 34, 38, 42, 43, 44, 45
 – Act of Union 43, 44
 – British North America Act 44
 – Confederation 44, 45
 – Lower Canada 13, 43, 44
 – rebellions (1837) 43, 44
 – Rupert's Land 45
 – Upper Canada 13, 43, 44
Carnegie, Andrew 38
Carpetbaggers 32
Carver, George Washington 38
Catlin, George 14, 40
Centennial Exhibition 38, 39
Charbonneau, Toussaint 10
Chile 16
China/Chinese 36, 44
Chinese Exclusion Act 36
Chisholm, Jesse 34
Civil Rights Act 32
Civil War 5, 7, 22, 23, 26, 27, 28, 29, 30, 31, 32, 35, 40
Clark, William 10, 11, 40
Clemens, Samuel Langhorne 40
Cody, William Frederick 35
Cole, Thomas 40
Confederate States, the (Confederacy) 5, 7, 28, 29, 30, 31
Congress 12, 13, 14, 19, 23, 30, 32, 37
Cooper, James Fenimore 40
Corps of Discovery 10
Costilla, Miguel Hidalgo y 16
cotton 7, 22, 24, 25, 26, 28, 38
cowboys 34
Crane, Stephen 40
Crazy Horse (Chief) 35
Creek War 14, 15
Crockett, Davy 17
Cuba 39
Custer, George Armstrong (General) 35

Davis, Jefferson (President) 28
de Bore, Etienne 23

Decatur, Stephen 9
Dewey, George (Commodore) 39
Doughty, Thomas 40
Douglas, Thomas (5th Earl of Selkirk) 42
Douglass, Frederick 40
Durand, Asher 40

Eastman, George 39
Edison, Thomas Alva 38, 39
Ellis Island 37
Emancipation Proclamation/Act 30, 31, 33
Embargo Act 12
Emerson, Ralph Waldo 41
England 8
Erie Canal 26

First Nations 42, 45
FitzGibbon, James (Lieutenant) 13
Fort Clatsop 11
Fort Sumter 28
France/French 6, 8, 9, 10, 12, 42, 44
French, Daniel Chester 40
Fugitive Slave Law 24, 25, 26, 27
fur traders/trappers 20, 42, 43

Garrison, William Lloyd 26, 27
George III (King of England) 8
Germany 37
Geronimo (Chief) 34, 35
Gettysburg Address 30
gold 18, 20, 34, 36, 38
Grant, Ulysses S. (General and President) 29, 31, 32
Great Plains 6
Green Corn festival 14
Guam 39
Guerrero, Vicente 17

Hamilton, Alexander (Founding Father) 8
Hammond, James H. (Senator) 22
Harrison, William Henry (General) 12
Homestead Act 35, 37
Hooker, Joe (General) 30
Houston, Sam 17
Howe, Elias 26
Hudson River School 40
Hudson's Bay Company 42, 43, 45

immigrants 6, 7, 26, 30, 36, 37, 38

Immigration Act 37
Indian Removal Act 14, 18, 19
Inuit 42
Ireland/Irish 36, 37
Iroquoian language 14
Italy 36, 37
Iturbide, Agustin de (Emperor) 16, 17

Jackson, Andrew (General and President) 14, 19
Jackson, Thomas "Stonewall" (General) 30
Jacobs, Harriet 40
James, Frank 34
James, Jesse 34, 35
Jefferson, Thomas (President) 6, 8, 9, 10, 12
Jerome, Leonard 32
Jews 37
Jim Crow laws 32
Johnson, Andrew (President) 32
Joplin, Scott 40, 41
Joseph (Chief) 34

Kansas-Nebraska Act 23, 24
Key, Francis Scott 13
King, Martin Luther 41
Ku Klux Klan 32

lacrosse 14
Lambton, John (1st Earl of Durham) 44
Lawrence, James (Captain) 12
Lee, Robert E. (General) 29, 30, 31
Lewis, Meriwether 10, 11
Libya 9
Lincoln, Abraham (President) 7, 28, 30, 31, 40
Louisiana Purchase/Territory 5, 6, 10, 14
Lowell, Francis Cabot 26

Macdonald, John A. (Prime Minister) 44
Macdonnell, Miles 42
Mackenzie, William Lyon 43
Marshall, James W. 20
McClellan, George B. (General) 29
McCormick, Cyrus H. 44
McGill, James 42
Meade, George G. (General) 30
Mediterranean Sea 9

Métis 42
Mexico 5, 6, 16, 17
   – Mexican War 16, 17
   – war of independence 16, 17
Military Reconstruction Act 32
Missouri Compromise, the 24
Monroe Doctrine 16
Monroe, James (President) 16
Mormons 19
Morocco 9
Mott, Lucretia Coffin 26
Mounties, the 45
Muskogean language 14

Native American Confederation 13, 14
Native Americans/peoples (*see also* First Nations) 5, 6, 10, 11, 13, 14, 15, 16, 18, 19, 21, 34, 35, 40, 42
   – Apaches 34, 35
   – Cherokee (people and language) 14, 15, 18, 19
   – Cheyenne 35
   – Chickasaw 14
   – Chocktaw 14
   – Creek 14, 15
   – five "civilized" tribes 14, 18
   – Hidatsa 11
   – Iroquois 18
   – Navajo 35
   – Nez Percé 34, 35
   – Plains 6, 40
   – Seminole 14, 18
   – Shawnee 12, 13, 15
   – Shoshone 10, 11
   – Sioux 34, 35
New York 26, 27, 30, 31, 32, 36, 37, 40
North West Company 42, 43

Oregon Trail 20
Otis, Elisha 26
outlaws 34

Papineau, Louis Joseph 43
Pemberton, John Styth 39
Peninsular Campaign 29, 30
Perry, Oliver (Captain) 13
Philippines 39
Pickett, George E. (General)
plantations 7, 22, 23, 24, 25, 26, 41
Poland 36
Pony Express 21
Presidents
   – Adams, John 8
   – Davis, Jefferson 28

   – Grant, Ulysses S. 29, 31, 32
   – Jackson, Andrew 14, 19
   – Jefferson, Thomas 6, 8, 9, 10, 12
   – Johnson, Andrew 32
   – Lincoln, Abraham 7, 28, 30, 31, 40
   – Monroe, James 16
   – van Buren 18
Puerto Rico 39

Quasi War 8

ragtime 41
railways (railroads) 7, 21, 33, 35, 36, 37, 42, 44
Reconstruction era 32, 33
Red River Settlement 42
Red Sticks 14, 15
reservations 6, 34, 35
Rillieux, Norbert 23
Roebling, John 37
Ross, John (Chief) 18
Russia 36

Sacagawea 10, 11
Saint-Gaudens, Augustus 40
Santa Anna 16
Scalawags 32
Scandinavia 36, 37
Scotland/Scottish 38, 39, 42
Scott, Winfield (General) 17
Secord, James 13
Secord, Laura Ingersoll 13
Seneca Falls Convention 26
Sequoyah (George Guess) 14, 15
Sherman, William Tecumseh (General) 31
Shreve, Henry Miller 23
Singer, Isaac 27
Sitting Bull (Chief) 35
slaves/slavery 7, 8, 14, 18, 22, 23, 24, 25, 26, 27, 28, 30, 31, 32, 33, 40
Smith, Joseph 19
Somers, Richard 8
Spain 5, 6, 16, 17, 39
Spanish-American War, the 39
Stanton, Elizabeth Cady 26
steamboats 23
steel 38
Stowe, Harriet Beecher 26, 27
sugar cane 7, 22, 23, 39
Sutter, John 20

Tariff of Abominations 23
Taylor, Zachary (General) 17

Tecumseh (Chief) 12, 13, 14, 15
Tenskwatawa 12
Texas 16, 34, 37
   – missions 16
   – war of independence 16, 17
textile mills 26
Thoreau, Henry David 41
tobacco 22, 31
Trail of Tears 18, 19
Transcendentalists 40, 41
Travis, William B. (Colonel) 17
Treaties
   – Adams-Onis 17
   – Fort Jackson 14
   – Ghent 13
   – Guadalupe-Hidalgo 17
   – New Echota 18
   – Oregon Boundary 44
   – Paris 39
   – Reciprocity 44
Tripoli 9
Tripolitania 9
Tubman, Harriet "Moses" 24, 25
Twain, Mark 40

Underground Railroad 24, 25
Union, the 7, 28, 29, 30, 31, 32

van Buren, Martin (President) 18
Vanderbilt, Alice 39
Venezuela 16

War of 1812 9, 12, 13, 14, 42
Weatherford, William (Chief Red Eagle) 14
Webster, Noah 40
Wells Fargo 21
Whitman, Marcus 20
Whitman, Walt 27
Whitney, Eli 8, 22, 24
Wild West 34, 34

XYZ Affair 8

Young, Brigham 19